THE *Succulent* BITE

THE *Succulent* BITE

60+
Easy Recipes for
Over-the-Top Desserts

NICO NORENA

Founder of The Succulent Bite

PAGE STREET
PUBLISHING CO.

PAGE STREET
PUBLISHING CO.

Copyright © 2022 Nico Norena

First published in 2022 by

Page Street Publishing Co.

27 Congress Street, Suite 1511

Salem, MA 01970

www.pagestreetpublishing.com

26   25   24   23   22   1   2   3   4   5

ISBN-13: 978-1-64567-569-3

ISBN-10: 1-64567-569-6

Library of Congress Control Number: 2021950897

Cover and book design by Rosie Stewart for Page Street Publishing Co.

Photography by Anthony Nader. Photograph on page 2 by Phraa.

Food Styling by Sarah Lucia Tafur

Printed and bound in the United States

DEDICATION

To my parents, Ariana, my sister, my friends and all of
my fans. Thank you for making this possible.

CONTENTS

INTRODUCTION

What's up everyone! My name is Nico Norena, and I am the founder of The Succulent Bite®, a food and lifestyle channel across social media that shares mouthwatering food content and works with global consumer brands like Burger King®, Betty Crocker, Kellogg's® and Snickers® to create tailored marketing campaigns to go live on @succulentbite. I am a passionate foodie, full-time creator and entrepreneur. My journey began six years ago when I first opened up all my social media accounts and began exploring the food world. But it was only in 2020 when I decided to pursue my career as a content creator and entrepreneur full time! This had always been my dream, so after years of development and preparation, I finally took the step! Today, I love creating easy recipes at home for you to try out and enjoy, many of which you may have seen across @succulentbite social channels!

This book is a collection of my favorite recipes. Wherever you choose to enjoy them—at home with family or elsewhere with friends—my hope is that these treats bring joy to you and those close to you. From cheesecakes to quick desserts and even ice cream, these are evergreen recipes that you'll love! Whether you follow the recipes exactly or you use them to create your own twist, I am very happy you now have a piece of The Succulent Bite with you! I hope you enjoy, and make sure to tag us when you try some of these out!

As always, cheers!

ICE CREAM *Fix*

Walking down the ice cream aisle, you see pints of vanilla, chocolate and maybe even the occasional strawberry. Opening the store cooler, you try to decide what flavor you'll choose this week. I'm here to tell you that you don't have to decide between boring vanilla or trite chocolate. You don't even have to settle for the same old blue or pink boxed ice cream cakes.

With a few basic ingredients you can create a world of creamy flavors on your own. Most of the ice cream recipes in this book start off with a base composed of heavy cream, vanilla extract and sweetened condensed milk. From there we add the personality, which is when a simple cream becomes a sassy concoction of dulce de leche (page 42), or Oreo® (page 22) or cold brew (page 25). Don't be afraid to experiment and get creative! Make your life and your home freezer more flavorful with my favorite ice cream and ice cream cake recipes.

CARAMELIZED BANANA ICE CREAM

This is a monkey's favorite ice cream, and now it'll be yours too! Its combination of silky cream and crunchy graham crackers creates a simple yet sophisticated scoop. This flavorful, rich and homemade sweet will make your friends and family go bananas.

Yields 6 servings

In a large bowl, add the heavy cream, condensed milk and vanilla. Using an electric hand mixer on high speed, whip the ingredients in circular motions. To avoid overmixing, you can reduce the mixer speed from high to medium after about 4 minutes of whipping. Once the mix has almost doubled in volume and has that fluffy texture, which should take about 2 minutes, you can stop.

While mixing, if you notice the mix begins to break, turn off the electric mixer and mix by hand slowly to reincorporate the cream base.

In a skillet over medium heat, add the banana, sugar and bourbon. Gently stir the ingredients until they become golden; this should take about 5 minutes. Let the caramelized banana cool, then gently fold it into the cream mixture.

Add the crackers to the mixture, and mix all the ingredients with an electric mixer at medium speed for about 1 minute. Place the mixture in a 6-cup (1,440-ml) freezer-safe glass container with a lid. (I prefer round containers, as they make it easier to scoop the ice cream later.) Freeze the mixture overnight; once it's hardened, scoop and serve in a bowl or ice cream cone.

INGREDIENTS

2 cups (480 ml) heavy cream

1 (14-oz [397-g]) can sweetened condensed milk

1 tbsp (15 ml) vanilla extract

1 banana, sliced

¼ cup (50 g) white granulated sugar

3 tbsp (45 ml) bourbon

3 graham crackers, crushed

SHORTBREAD COOKIE ICE CREAM

Do you have some leftover shortbread cookies from that box you bought a couple months ago? You can mix them right into this ice cream and enjoy them all over again! This ice cream is creamy, easy to make and will impress any cookie lover!

Yields 6 servings

In a large bowl, add the heavy cream, condensed milk and vanilla. Using an electric hand mixer on high speed, whip the ingredients in circular motions. To avoid overmixing, you can reduce the mixer speed from high to medium after about 4 minutes of whipping. Once the mix has almost doubled in volume and has that fluffy texture, which should take about 2 minutes, you can stop.

While mixing, if you notice the mix begins to break, turn off the electric mixer and mix by hand slowly to reincorporate the cream base.

Add the cookies to the mixture, and fold the ingredients together. Place the mixture in a 6-cup (1,440-ml) freezer-safe glass container with a lid. (I prefer round containers, as they make it easier to scoop the ice cream later.) Freeze the mixture overnight; once it's hardened, scoop and serve in a bowl or ice cream cone.

INGREDIENTS

2 cups (480 ml) heavy cream

1 (14-oz [397-g]) can sweetened condensed milk

1 tbsp (15 ml) vanilla extract

15 shortbread cookies, crushed

CHIPS AHOY!® CHOCOLATE ICE CREAM

Ready to take the sweet satisfaction of chocolate to the next level?
This chocolate lover's dessert is a fun twist on a classic treat and a
great excuse to buy another box of Chips Ahoy!® cookies.
It's creamy, cool and hits the spot every time.

Yields 6 servings

In a large bowl, add the heavy cream, condensed milk and vanilla. Using an electric hand mixer on high speed, whip the ingredients in circular motions. To avoid overmixing, you can reduce the mixer speed from high to medium after about 4 minutes of whipping. Once the mix has almost doubled in volume and has that fluffy texture, which should take about 2 minutes, you can stop.

While mixing, if you notice the mix begins to break, turn off the electric mixer and mix by hand slowly to reincorporate the cream base.

Add the cookies and the cocoa powder to the mixture, and fold the ingredients together. Place the mixture in a 6-cup (1,440-ml) freezer-safe glass container with a lid. (I prefer round containers, as they make it easier to scoop the ice cream later.) Freeze the mixture overnight; once it's hardened, scoop and serve in a bowl or ice cream cone.

INGREDIENTS

2 cups (480 ml) heavy cream

1 (14-oz [397-g]) can sweetened condensed milk

1 tbsp (15 ml) vanilla extract

13 chocolate chip cookies (I prefer Chips Ahoy! cookies), crushed

1½ tbsp (8 g) unsweetened cocoa powder

CHOCOLATE STRAWBERRY CHEESECAKE ICE CREAM

Calling all cheesecake lovers! This thick cream cheese batter revolutionizes the concept of velvety ice cream. Its chocolatey goodness and fresh strawberries combine to create one of my favorite treats from this collection.

Yields 6 servings

In a large bowl, add the cream cheese, cocoa powder, 4 of the chopped strawberries, vanilla and condensed milk. Using an electric hand mixer on high speed, whip the ingredients in circular motions until smooth. To avoid overmixing, you can reduce the mixer speed from high to medium after about 4 minutes of whipping. Once the mix is fully combined and creamy, which should take about 4 minutes, you can stop.

In a separate bowl, add the heavy cream and mix on high speed until peaks form. Next, add the whipped cream to the cream cheese mixture, folding gently to incorporate the ingredients.

Place the mixture in a 6-cup (1,440-ml) freezer-safe glass container with a lid. (I prefer round containers, as they make it easier to scoop the ice cream later.) Top the mixture with the remaining chopped strawberries. Freeze the mixture for at least 5 hours; once it's hardened, scoop and serve in a bowl or ice cream cone.

INGREDIENTS

8 oz (226 g) cream cheese

⅓ cup (32 g) unsweetened cocoa powder

6 large strawberries, chopped, divided (4 for the batter, 2 for garnish)

1 tbsp (15 ml) vanilla extract

1 (14-oz [397-g]) can sweetened condensed milk

2¼ cups (540 ml) heavy cream

MILK & CEREAL ICE CREAM

Breakfast for dinner? Better yet—breakfast for dessert! This recipe takes the joy of your morning cereal and puts it into a creamy treat. The crunchy flakes and the fluffy cream should definitely be the most important meal of your day.

Yields 2 servings

In a large bowl, add the heavy cream, condensed milk and vanilla. Using an electric hand mixer on high speed, whip the ingredients in circular motions. To avoid overmixing, you can reduce the mixer speed from high to medium after about 4 minutes of whipping. Once the mix has almost doubled in volume and has that fluffy texture, which should take about 2 minutes, you can stop.

While mixing, if you notice the mix begins to break, turn off the electric mixer and mix by hand slowly to reincorporate the cream base.

Next, carefully mix in the cereal and sprinkles. Once the ingredients are incorporated, split the mixture between two ramekins, and freeze them uncovered for at least 3 hours. Enjoy the ice cream right out of the ramekin. This recipe was made for two individual portions, but if you'd like to make a larger batch, double the ingredients up!

INGREDIENTS

1 cup (240 ml) heavy cream

7 oz (198 g) sweetened condensed milk

½ tbsp (8 ml) vanilla extract

1½ cups (59 g) sugar-coated cornflakes cereal (I prefer Frosted Flakes®)

⅓ cup (64 g) rainbow sprinkles

OREO® ICE CREAM

This is a classic ice cream recipe made even simpler. With only four ingredients, a yummy swirl of cookies and cream is created. It's smooth, crunchy and a trusted treat that will keep you coming back for more.

Yields 6 servings

In a large bowl, add the heavy cream, condensed milk and vanilla. Using an electric hand mixer on high speed, whip the ingredients in circular motions. To avoid overmixing, you can reduce the mixer speed from high to medium after about 4 minutes of whipping. Once the mix has almost doubled in volume and has that fluffy texture, you can stop.

While mixing, if you notice the mix begins to break, turn off the electric mixer and mix by hand slowly to reincorporate the cream base.

Add the cookies to the mixture, and fold the ingredients together. Place the mixture in a 6-cup (1,440-ml) freezer-safe glass container with a lid. (I prefer round containers, as they make it easier to scoop the ice cream later.) Freeze the mixture overnight; once it's hardened, scoop and serve in a bowl or ice cream cone.

INGREDIENTS

2 cups (480 ml) heavy cream

1 (14-oz [397-g]) can sweetened condensed milk

1 tbsp (15 ml) vanilla extract

13 chocolate sandwich cookies (I prefer Oreo cookies), crushed

COLD BREW DULCE DE LECHE ICE CREAM

Looking for a sweet way to get your daily caffeine fix? Then this recipe is for you! This ice cream's light coffee taste and rich dulce de leche swirls are sure to pack a flavorful punch. This dynamic duo certainly won't disappoint.

Yields 6 servings

In a large bowl, add the heavy cream, condensed milk and vanilla. Using an electric hand mixer on high speed, whip the ingredients in circular motions. To avoid overmixing, you can reduce the mixer speed from high to medium after about 4 minutes of whipping. Once the mix has almost doubled in volume and has that fluffy texture, which should take about 2 minutes, you can stop.

While mixing, if you notice the mix begins to break, turn off the electric mixer and mix by hand slowly to reincorporate the cream base.

Next, carefully mix in the coffee and chocolate to the cream mixture, and whip the ingredients together. Place the mixture in a 6-cup (1,440-ml) freezer-safe glass container with a lid. (I prefer round containers, as they make it easier to scoop the ice cream later.) Freeze the mixture for at least 6 hours; once it's hardened, scoop and serve in a bowl or ice cream cone topped with dulce de leche.

INGREDIENTS

2 cups (480 ml) heavy cream

1 (14-oz [397-g]) can sweetened condensed milk

1 tbsp (15 ml) vanilla extract

½ cup (120 ml) cold brew coffee (or 3 [1-oz (30-ml)] espresso shots, chilled)

3.5 oz (98 g) dark chocolate, chopped

3 tbsp (59 g) dulce de leche, for topping

BISCOFF® COOKIES ICE CREAM

Not only does every coffee need a Biscoff®, but so does every ice cream. This tiny but mighty cookie's deep spice and caramel flavor balances perfectly with the velvety vanilla ice cream. If this is your favorite cookie, then this is your new favorite dessert.

Yields 6 servings

In a large bowl, add the heavy cream, condensed milk and vanilla. Using an electric hand mixer on high speed, whip the ingredients in circular motions. To avoid overmixing, you can reduce the mixer speed from high to medium after about 4 minutes of whipping. Once the mix has almost doubled in volume and has that fluffy texture, which should take about 2 minutes, you can stop.

While mixing, if you notice the mix begins to break, turn off the electric mixer and mix by hand slowly to reincorporate the cream base.

Next, add the cookies and fold the ingredients together. Place the mixture in a 6-cup (1,440-ml) freezer-safe glass container with a lid. (I prefer round containers, as they make it easier to scoop the ice cream later.) Freeze the mixture for at least 6 hours; once it's hardened, scoop and serve in a bowl or ice cream cone.

INGREDIENTS

2 cups (480 ml) heavy cream

1 (14-oz [397-g]) can sweetened condensed milk

1 tbsp (15 ml) vanilla extract

4 oz (113 g) speculoos cookies (I prefer Biscoff cookies), crushed

NESQUIK® ICE CREAM

The unique flavor of Nesquik® takes me back to my childhood. If you're like me and looking for a way to be transported back in time, this recipe is for you. The best part is you don't even have to choose between strawberry and chocolate flavors . . . you can have both!

Yields 6 servings

In a large bowl, add the heavy cream, condensed milk and vanilla. Using an electric hand mixer on high speed, whip the ingredients in circular motions. To avoid overmixing, you can reduce the mixer speed from high to medium after about 4 minutes of whipping. Once the mix has almost doubled in volume and has that fluffy texture, which should take about 2 minutes, you can stop.

While mixing, if you notice the mix begins to break, turn off the electric mixer and mix by hand slowly to reincorporate the cream base.

Divide the mixture into two medium-sized bowls. In one bowl, add the chocolate milk powder and stir gently until it is fully incorporated. In the remaining bowl, add the strawberry milk powder and stir gently until it is fully incorporated.

Pour the two ice cream flavors into a 6-cup (1,440-ml) freezer-safe glass container with a lid. (I prefer round containers, as they make it easier to scoop the ice cream later.) Make sure to pour each flavor on opposite ends of the container so the colors do not mix together; you could also use a plastic divider for this step. Freeze the mixture overnight; once it's hardened, scoop and serve in a bowl or ice cream cone with chocolate syrup.

INGREDIENTS

2¼ cups (540 ml) heavy cream

1 (14-oz [397-g]) can sweetened condensed milk

1 tsp vanilla extract

3 tbsp (21 g) chocolate milk powder (I prefer chocolate Nesquik)

3 tbsp (21 g) strawberry milk powder (I prefer strawberry Nesquik)

⅓ cup (80 ml) chocolate syrup, for topping

DARK CHOCOLATE RASPBERRY ICE CREAM

Picture this: it's raspberry season, and the markets are selling those red, juicy berries. What do you make with them? Easy answer: Dark Chocolate Raspberry Ice Cream! Its perfect balance between fruity cream and dark chocolate pieces is simply irresistible.

Yields 6 servings

In a blender, add the raspberries, sugar and water, and blend to form a paste. Set the paste aside.

In a large bowl, add the heavy cream, condensed milk and vanilla. Using an electric hand mixer on high speed, whip the ingredients in circular motions. To avoid overmixing, you can reduce the mixer speed from high to medium after about 4 minutes of whipping. Once the mix has almost doubled in volume and has that fluffy texture, which should take about 2 minutes, you can stop.

While mixing, if you notice the mix begins to break, turn off the electric mixer and mix by hand slowly to reincorporate the cream base.

Next, add in the raspberry paste and chocolate to the cream mixture, and fold the ingredients together. Place the mixture in a 6-cup (1,440-ml) freezer-safe glass container with a lid. (I prefer round containers, as they make it easier to scoop the ice cream later.) Freeze the mixture for at least 5 hours; once it's hardened, scoop and serve in a bowl or ice cream cone.

INGREDIENTS

6 oz (170 g) raspberries

⅓ cup (66 g) white granulated sugar

¼ cup (60 ml) water, warm

2¼ cups (540 ml) heavy cream

1 (14-oz [397-g]) can sweetened condensed milk

1 tsp vanilla extract

3.5 oz (98 g) dark chocolate, chopped

OREO® GRAHAM CRACKERS CHEESECAKE ICE CREAM

This isn't just any ice cream—it's Oreo Graham Cracker Cheesecake Ice Cream. Meaning it has Oreo chunks, graham cracker crunch and thick, velvety cream. In other words, the O in Oreo Graham Cracker Cheesecake Ice Cream stands for "Oh wow!"

Yields 6 servings

In a large bowl, add the cream cheese, condensed milk and vanilla. Using an electric hand mixer on high speed, whip the ingredients in circular motions. Next add your heavy cream and keep mixing. To avoid overmixing, you can reduce the mixer speed from high to medium after about 4 minutes of whipping. Once the mix has almost doubled in volume and has that fluffy texture, which should take about 2 minutes, you can stop.

While mixing, if you notice the mix begins to break, turn off the electric mixer and mix by hand slowly to reincorporate the cream base.

Next, add in the crackers and cookies and fold into the mixture carefully. Place the mixture in a 6-cup (1,440-ml) freezer-safe glass container with a lid. (I prefer round containers, as they make it easier to scoop the ice cream later.) Freeze the mixture for at least 5 hours; once it's hardened, scoop and serve in a bowl or ice cream cone.

INGREDIENTS

8 oz (226 g) cream cheese

1 (14-oz [397-g]) can sweetened condensed milk

1 tbsp (15 ml) vanilla extract

2¼ cups (540 ml) heavy cream

2 graham crackers, lightly crumbled

10 chocolate sandwich cookies (I prefer Oreo cookies), chopped

CHOCOLATE POUND CAKE ICE CREAM

I'm sure you've had pound cake with ice cream, but have you ever had pound cake ice cream? Let me make your life better with this smooth, spongy dessert. Its chocolatey chunks of cake and thick cream are sure to make your heart pound.

Yields 6 servings

In a large bowl, add the heavy cream, condensed milk and vanilla. Using an electric hand mixer on high speed, whip the ingredients in circular motions. To avoid overmixing, you can reduce the mixer speed from high to medium after about 4 minutes of whipping. Once the mix has almost doubled in volume and has that fluffy texture, which should take about 2 minutes, you can stop.

While mixing, if you notice the mix begins to break, turn off the electric mixer and mix by hand slowly to reincorporate the cream base.

Next, add the cake to the cream mixture, and mix the ingredients together carefully.

Place the mixture in a 6-cup (1,440-ml) freezer-safe glass container with a lid. (I prefer round containers, as they make it easier to scoop the ice cream later.) Freeze the mixture for at least 5 hours; once it's hardened, scoop and serve in a bowl or ice cream cone and top with chocolate syrup.

INGREDIENTS

2¼ cups (540 ml) heavy cream

1 (14-oz [397-g]) can sweetened condensed milk

1 tbsp (15 ml) vanilla extract

7 oz (198 g) chocolate pound cake (about 2 slices), chopped

3 tbsp (45 ml) chocolate syrup, for topping

PUMPKIN SPICE ICE CREAM

I live in Miami, where fall isn't composed of changing leaves and a cool breeze. Fall means high temperatures and sweaty foreheads. As a result, Florida's fall festivities don't include things like pumpkin spice lattes, but they do have things like Pumpkin Spice Ice Cream. Some say Floridians have more fun, and in this case I agree.

Yields 6 servings

In a large bowl, add the heavy cream, condensed milk and vanilla. Using an electric hand mixer on high speed, whip the ingredients in circular motions. To avoid overmixing, you can reduce the mixer speed from high to medium after about 4 minutes of whipping. Once the mix has almost doubled in volume and has that fluffy texture, which should take about 2 minutes, you can stop.

While mixing, if you notice the mix begins to break, turn off the electric mixer and mix by hand slowly to reincorporate the cream base.

Next, add the pumpkin, nutmeg, ginger, cinnamon and allspice to the cream mixture, and mix the ingredients together on medium speed.

Place the mixture in a 6-cup (1,440-ml) freezer-safe glass container with a lid. (I prefer round containers, as they make it easier to scoop the ice cream later.) Freeze the mixture for at least 6 hours; once it's hardened, scoop and serve in a bowl or ice cream cone.

INGREDIENTS

2 cups (480 ml) heavy cream

1 (14-oz [397-g]) can sweetened condensed milk

1 tbsp (15 ml) vanilla extract

¾ cup (184 g) pumpkin puree

1 tsp nutmeg

1 tsp ground ginger

1 tsp cinnamon

1 tsp allspice

NUTELLA® CHIPS AHOY!® ICE CREAM

This cookies-and-cream Nutella® recipe is a chocolate lover's dream.
Its crunchy Chips Ahoy! pieces and smooth cream are a match made
in heaven. It's a holy treat made for every day of the week,
not just Sundays.

Yields 6 servings

In a large bowl, add the heavy cream, condensed milk and vanilla. Using an electric hand mixer on high speed, whip the ingredients in circular motions. To avoid overmixing, you can reduce the mixer speed from high to medium after about 4 minutes of whipping. Once the mix has almost doubled in volume and has that fluffy texture, which should take about 2 minutes, you can stop.

While mixing, if you notice the mix begins to break, turn off the electric mixer and mix by hand slowly to reincorporate the cream base.

Next, add the hazelnut cocoa spread and cookies to the cream mixture, and mix the ingredients together carefully.

Place the mixture in a 6-cup (1,440-ml) freezer-safe glass container with a lid. (I prefer round containers, as they make it easier to scoop the ice cream later.) Freeze the mixture for at least 4 hours; once it's hardened, scoop and serve in a bowl or ice cream cone.

INGREDIENTS

2 cups (480 ml) heavy cream

1 (14-oz [397-g]) can sweetened condensed milk

1 tbsp (15 ml) vanilla extract

5 tbsp (93 g) hazelnut cocoa spread (I prefer Nutella)

12 chocolate chip cookies (I prefer Chips Ahoy! cookies), chopped

RED VELVET POUND CAKE ICE CREAM

If you're like me then you associate the color red with hearts and love. Specifically, love for this Red Velvet Pound Cake Ice Cream. Its crispy cake and red velvety cream is a fun and delicious way to make a dessert.

Yields 6 servings

In a large bowl, add the heavy cream, condensed milk, cocoa powder, vanilla and food coloring. Using an electric hand mixer on high speed, whip the ingredients in circular motions. To avoid overmixing, you can reduce the mixer speed from high to medium after about 4 minutes of whipping. Once the mix has almost doubled in volume and has that fluffy texture, which should take about 2 minutes, you can stop.

While mixing, if you notice the mix begins to break, turn off the electric mixer and mix by hand slowly to reincorporate the cream base.

Next, carefully fold the pound cake into the mixture.

Place the mixture in a 6-cup (1,440-ml) freezer-safe glass container with a lid. (I prefer round containers, as they make it easier to scoop the ice cream later.) Freeze the mixture overnight; once it's hardened, scoop and serve in a bowl or ice cream cone.

INGREDIENTS

2 cups (480 ml) heavy cream

1 (14-oz [397-g]) can sweetened condensed milk

2 tbsp (10 g) unsweetened cocoa powder

1 tbsp (15 ml) vanilla extract

1 tbsp (15 ml) red food coloring

8 oz (226 g) pound cake, cubed

CHOCOLATE CHUNK DULCE DE LECHE

Anything with "Chocolate Chunk" in its name is guaranteed to be good, but when it has both "Chocolate Chunk" and "Dulce de Leche," it's guaranteed to be extraordinary. I'm not telling you to judge a book by its cover, but this is a really appealing cover.

Yields 6 servings

In a large bowl, add the heavy cream, dulce de leche and vanilla. Using an electric hand mixer on high speed, whip the ingredients in circular motions until creamy. It will be done once the mix has almost doubled in volume and has that fluffy texture. If you notice the cream starts to break, stop the mixer and gently reincorporate the cream by hand.

Next, carefully fold the chocolate and cookies into the mixture.

Place the mixture in a 6-cup (1,440-ml) freezer-safe glass container with a lid. (I prefer round containers, as they make it easier to scoop the ice cream later.) Freeze for at least 4 hours; once it's hardened, scoop and serve in a bowl or ice cream cone.

INGREDIENTS

2 cups (480 ml) heavy cream

1 (14-oz [396-g]) can dulce de leche

1 tbsp (15 ml) vanilla extract

4 oz (113 g) dark chocolate, shaved

3 Spanish tea cookies (I prefer Goya® Maria Cookies), crumbled

OREO® ICE CREAM CAKE

This is basically your favorite cookie in an XXXL version! It has triple the flavor and triple the fun. The crunchy chocolatey shell and the creamy vanilla interior are going to make you wish you had three more. Two for later and one for later, later.

Yields 8 servings

To make the crust, in a large bowl, add the cookies and butter. Mix the ingredients until well combined, then halve the mixture.

Place one half of the mixture in a 9-inch (23-cm) cake pan, and press the mix into the bottom of the pan until it is compact and spread across the entire bottom to the edges. Place the pan in the freezer to harden.

Place the other half of the mixture in a 9-inch (23-cm) springform cake pan. This will be the bottom crust, meaning you will add the ice cream mix on top of this crust. Set this crust aside.

To make the ice cream, in a large bowl, add the heavy cream, condensed milk and vanilla. Using an electric hand mixer on high speed, whip the ingredients in circular motions until creamy. Once the mix has almost doubled in volume and has that fluffy texture, which should take about 2 minutes, you can stop.

While mixing, if you notice the mix begins to break, turn off the electric mixer and mix by hand slowly to reincorporate the cream base.

Add the ice cream mixture on top of the bottom crust in the springform pan, spreading it out evenly across the top. Then, place the frozen crust on top of the mixture. Freeze the ice cream cake overnight to harden.

INGREDIENTS

CRUST

54 chocolate sandwich cookies (I prefer Oreo cookies), finely crushed

10 tbsp (140 g) unsalted butter, melted

ICE CREAM

5 cups (1,200 ml) heavy cream

1 (14-oz [397-g]) can sweetened condensed milk

2 tbsp (30 ml) vanilla extract

SNICKERS® ICE CREAM CAKE

On a hot summer's day, one Snickers ice cream bar is not going to cut it but a Snickers Ice Cream Cake just might! With its dulce de leche cream and chewy Snickers pieces, cooling down will feel like a blessing.

Yields 8 servings

To make the crust, in a large bowl, add the graham snacks and butter. Mix the ingredients until well combined, then halve the mixture.

Place one half of the mixture in a 9-inch (23-cm) cake pan, and press the mix into the bottom of the pan until it is compact and spread across the entire bottom to the edges. Place the pan in the freezer to harden.

Place the other half of the mixture in a 9-inch (23-cm) springform cake pan. This will be the bottom crust, meaning you will add the ice cream mix on top of this crust. Set this crust aside.

To make the ice cream, in a large bowl, add the heavy cream, dulce de leche, candy bars and vanilla. Using an electric hand mixer on high speed, whip the ingredients in circular motions. Once the mix has almost doubled in volume and has that fluffy texture, which should take about 2 minutes, you can stop.

Add the ice cream mixture on top of the bottom crust in the springform pan, spreading it out evenly across the top. Then, place the frozen crust on top of the mixture. Freeze the ice cream cake overnight to harden.

Decorate your cake with extra chopped candy bars (if using)!

INGREDIENTS

CRUST

2 (10-oz [283-g]) boxes chocolate graham snacks (I prefer chocolate Teddy Grahams®), finely crushed

10 tbsp (140 g) unsalted butter, melted

ICE CREAM

5 cups (1,200 ml) heavy cream

1 (14-oz [396-g]) can dulce de leche

3 (1.86-oz [52.7-g]) chocolate nougat candy bars (I prefer Snickers bars), crushed, plus more for topping

2 tbsp (30 ml) vanilla extract

CHIPS AHOY!® ICE CREAM CAKE

Ahoy, ahoy! If you're a pirate looking for gold, look no further. This recipe—with its crumbly cookie crust and creamy sweet filling—is a hidden treasure. Not to mention, it's packed with chocolate chips and dulce de leche.

Yields 8 servings

To make the crust, in a large bowl, add the cookies and butter. Mix the ingredients until well combined, then halve the mixture.

Place one half of the mixture in a 9-inch (23-cm) cake pan, and press the mix into the bottom of the pan until it is compact and spread across the entire bottom to the edges. Place the pan in the freezer to harden.

Place the other half of the mixture in a 9-inch (23-cm) springform cake pan. This will be the bottom crust, meaning you will add the ice cream mix on top of this crust. Set this crust aside.

To make the ice cream, in a large bowl, add the heavy cream, dulce de leche and vanilla. Using an electric hand mixer on high speed, whip the ingredients in circular motions. Once the mix has almost doubled in volume and has that fluffy texture, which should take about 2 minutes, you can stop.

Next, add the chocolate chips and fold in carefully. Add the ice cream mixture on top of the bottom crust in the springform pan, spreading it out evenly across the top. Then, place the frozen crust on top of the mixture. Freeze the ice cream cake overnight to harden.

Decorate with extra chocolate chip cookies!

INGREDIENTS

CRUST

60 chocolate chip cookies (I prefer Chips Ahoy! cookies), finely crushed, plus more for topping

10 tbsp (140 g) unsalted butter, melted

ICE CREAM

5 cups (1,200 ml) heavy cream

1 (14-oz [396-g]) can dulce de leche

2 tbsp (30 ml) vanilla extract

1 cup (168 g) semisweet chocolate chips

NUTTER BUTTER® ICE CREAM CAKE

You are going to go nuts for this Nutter Butter® Ice Cream cake!
Its cookie sandwich is salty yet sweet, and its ice cream filling has
a subtle peanut butter taste. Who needs chocolate or jam when it's
already so delicious on its own?

Yields 8 servings

To make the crust, in a large bowl, add the cookies and butter. Mix the ingredients until well combined, then halve the mixture.

Place one half of the mixture in a 9-inch (23-cm) cake pan, and press the mix into the bottom of the pan until it is compact and spread across the entire bottom to the edges. Place the pan in the freezer to harden.

Place the other half of the mixture in a 9-inch (23-cm) springform cake pan. This will be the bottom crust, meaning you will add the ice cream mix on top of this crust. Set this crust aside.

To make the ice cream, in a large bowl, add the heavy cream, peanut butter, condensed milk and vanilla. Using an electric hand mixer on high speed, whip the ingredients in circular motions. Once the mix has almost doubled in volume and has that fluffy texture, which should take about 2 minutes, you can stop.

Add the ice cream mixture on top of the bottom crust in the springform pan, spreading it out evenly across the top. Then, place the frozen crust on top of the mixture. Freeze the ice cream cake overnight to harden.

Decorate with extra cookies (if using)!

INGREDIENTS

CRUST

60 peanut butter sandwich cookies (I prefer Nutter Butter cookies), finely crushed, plus more for topping

10 tbsp (140 g) unsalted butter, melted

ICE CREAM

5 cups (1,200 ml) heavy cream

4 tbsp (64 g) peanut butter

7 oz (198 g) sweetened condensed milk

2 tbsp (30 ml) vanilla extract

BISCOFF® COOKIES ICE CREAM CAKE

Is one small Biscoff cookie with your coffee not going to do it?
Two? What about an entire cake? I would go with the last option too.
This Biscoff Cookies Ice Cream Cake is packed with that signature
flavor you love, from the crispy cookie crust to the creamy
cookie butter filling.

Yields 8 servings

To make the crust, in a large bowl, add the cookies and butter. Mix the ingredients until well combined, then halve the mixture.

Place one half of the mixture in a 9-inch (23-cm) cake pan, and press the mix into the bottom of the pan until it is compact and spread across the entire bottom to the edges. Place the pan in the freezer to harden.

Place the other half of the mixture in a 9-inch (23-cm) springform cake pan. This will be the bottom crust, meaning you will add the ice cream mix on top of this crust. Set this crust aside.

To make the ice cream, in a large bowl, add the heavy cream, cookie butter, condensed milk and vanilla. Using an electric hand mixer on high speed, whip the ingredients in circular motions. Once the mix has almost doubled in volume and has that fluffy texture, which should take about 2 minutes, you can stop.

Add the ice cream mixture on top of the bottom crust in the springform pan, spreading it out evenly across the top. Then, place the frozen crust on top of the mixture. Freeze the ice cream cake overnight to harden.

Decorate with extra cookies (if using)!

INGREDIENTS

CRUST

64 speculoos cookies (I prefer Biscoff cookies), finely crushed, plus more for topping

10 tbsp (140 g) unsalted butter, melted

ICE CREAM

5 cups (1,200 ml) heavy cream

4 tbsp (60 g) cookie butter (I prefer Biscoff cookie butter)

7 oz (198 g) sweetened condensed milk

2 tbsp (30 ml) vanilla extract

Ultra-
CREAMY
CHEESECAKES

Cheesecakes may be among the most popular desserts worldwide! There are so many different ways to make cheesecake—from Japanese-style jiggly cheesecakes, to classic American cheesecakes and even Basque-style crustless cheesecakes. Each type brings an array of flavor and creativity to the table! In this chapter, I have compiled a list of some of my favorite cheesecake recipes and creations for you to indulge in at home! Creativity is one of my favorite aspects of baking cheesecakes. I see cheesecake as a white canvas onto which I can pour my favorite ingredients to create some mouthwatering concoctions!

RED VELVET NO-BAKE CHEESECAKE (OREO® CRUST!)

This love potion will make you fall head over heels. Its creamy consistency and chocolatey cookie crust is the sweetest way to someone's heart. Especially the hearts of cheesecake lovers!

Yields 8 servings

To make the crust, in a large bowl, add the cookies and butter. Mix the ingredients until well combined. Place the mixture in a 9-inch (23-cm) springform cake pan; make sure to spread the crust along the entire bottom of the pan to the edges. Freeze the pan for 15 minutes.

To make the cheesecake batter, in a large bowl, add the cream cheese and sugar. Using an electric hand mixer on high speed, whip the ingredients in circular motions until creamy.

Next, add the food coloring, cocoa powder and chocolate, and mix all the ingredients until they're fully incorporated.

In a separate bowl, add the heavy cream. Using an electric hand mixer on high speed, whip the cream in circular motions until creamy. It will be done once the mix has almost doubled in volume and has that fluffy texture. If you notice the cream start to break, stop the mixer and gently reincorporate the cream by hand.

Next, fold the whipped cream into the cream cheese mixture until well combined. Pour the mix on top of the prepared crust. Wrap the cheesecake and pan in aluminum foil, and place the pan in the refrigerator to set for at least 5 hours.

For the garnish, use a bowl to whip your cream, vanilla and sugar at high speed for about 1 minute until peaks form. Place a dollop on the top of your cheesecake and top with cookies!

INGREDIENTS

CRUST

23 chocolate sandwich cookies (I prefer Oreo cookies), crushed

5 tbsp (70 g) unsalted butter, melted

CHEESECAKE BATTER

32 oz (896 g) cream cheese, softened to room temperature

1 cup (120 g) confectioners' sugar

2 tsp (10 ml) red food coloring

2 tbsp (10 g) unsweetened cocoa powder

4 oz (113 g) white chocolate, melted

1 cup (240 ml) heavy cream

GARNISH (OPTIONAL)

½ cup (120 ml) heavy cream

½ tsp vanilla extract

2 tbsp (16 g) confectioners' sugar

2 chocolate sandwich cookies (I prefer Oreo cookies), cut in half

NUTELLA® OREO® CHEESECAKE

This recipe isn't for the faint of heart. Its velvety Nutella filling and crispy Oreo crust will make you go crazy. Yes, it's that insanely good, but don't take my word for it—try it out!

Yields 8 servings

Preheat the oven to 325°F (165°C). Then, take the bottom of the cake pan and evenly grease it.

To make the crust, in a large bowl, add the cookies and butter. Mix the ingredients until well combined. Place the mixture in a 9-inch (23-cm) springform cake pan; make sure to spread the crust along the entire bottom of the pan to the edges. Bake the crust for 15 minutes, then set it aside to cool. Keep the oven on.

To make the cheesecake batter, in a large bowl, add the cream cheese and sugar. Using an electric hand mixer on high speed, whip the ingredients in circular motions until creamy. Add in the eggs, vanilla and hazelnut cocoa spread, and continue to mix until the ingredients are incorporated.

Next, add the heavy cream. Mix the cream in on high speed until the mixture is fluffy; this should take about 5 minutes.

Wrap the outside of the cake pan in aluminum foil. Pour the cheesecake batter on top of the cooled crust. Take out a large baking pan, and fill it with about an inch (3 cm) of water. Gently place the cake pan inside the baking pan, and bake the cheesecake for 1 hour. Baking it like this will prevent the cheesecake from drying up.

When the cheesecake is done baking, remove from the oven and let the cheesecake cool for 1 hour at room temperature. Once the cheesecake cools to room temperature, wrap it while still in the pan with aluminum foil and place it in the refrigerator for 8 hours.

Decorate with hazelnut cocoa spread, hazelnuts and cookies (if desired), serve and enjoy!

INGREDIENTS

CRUST

28 chocolate sandwich cookies (I prefer Oreo cookies), finely crushed

7 tbsp (98 g) unsalted butter

CHEESECAKE BATTER

24 oz (680 g) cream cheese, softened to room temperature

½ cup (100 g) white granulated sugar

5 eggs

1 tbsp (15 ml) vanilla extract

2 cups (592 g) hazelnut cocoa spread (I prefer Nutella)

1 cup (240 ml) heavy cream

GARNISH (OPTIONAL)

½ cup (148 g) hazelnut cocoa spread (I prefer Nutella)

Roasted hazelnuts

8 chocolate sandwich cookies (I prefer Oreo cookies), cut in half

JAVA MONSTER® NO-BAKE CHEESECAKE

Try saying this three times fast: Java Monster® No-Bake Cheesecake. Better yet, try eating three cheesecakes! Trust me when I say that it won't take much effort. This Java Monster No-Bake Cheesecake's silky coffee taste and chocolate ganache will leave you begging for another slice.

Yields 8 servings

To make the crust, in a large bowl, add the cookies and butter. Mix the ingredients until well combined. Place the mixture in a 9-inch (23-cm) springform cake pan; make sure to spread the crust along the entire bottom of the pan to the edges. Freeze the pan for 30 minutes.

To make the cheesecake batter, in a large bowl, add the cream cheese. Using an electric hand mixer on high speed, whip the cream cheese until it's fluffy. Add in the energy drink, sour cream, granulated sugar, cream and cocoa powder. Mix until the ingredients are incorporated.

Pour the cheesecake batter on top of the cooled crust. Wrap the cheesecake and pan in aluminum foil, and refrigerate the cheesecake for at least 3 to 4 hours, but preferably overnight.

Before serving, make the ganache. In a medium-sized bowl, add the chocolate, confectioners' sugar, energy drink and heavy cream. Mix the ingredients until they are well combined. Just before serving, carefully pour the ganache onto the top of the cheesecake.

INGREDIENTS

CRUST

21 chocolate sandwich cookies (I prefer Oreo cookies), crushed

4 tbsp (56 g) unsalted butter

CHEESECAKE BATTER

16 oz (454 g) cream cheese, softened to room temperature

⅓ cup (80 ml) coffee-flavored energy drink (I prefer Java Monster's Loca Moca flavor)

⅓ cup (80 ml) sour cream

½ cup (100 g) white granulated sugar

⅓ cup (80 ml) heavy cream

1 tbsp (5 g) unsweetened cocoa powder

GANACHE

3.5 oz (98 g) dark chocolate, melted

1 cup (120 g) confectioners' sugar

¼ cup (60 ml) coffee-flavored energy drink (I prefer Java Monster's Loca Moca flavor)

2 tbsp (30 ml) heavy cream

BISCOFF® COOKIE BUTTER CHEESECAKE

Some say that an apple a day keeps the doctor away. I prefer the saying, a Biscoff Cookie Butter Cheesecake a day keeps the bad vibes away. The Biscoff cookie crust and cookie butter filling are the best kind of medication.

Yields 8 servings

Start by preheating the oven to 325°F (165°C). Then, take the bottom of the cake pan and evenly grease it.

To make the crust, in a large bowl, add the cookies and butter. Mix the ingredients until well combined. Place the mixture in a 9-inch (23-cm) cake pan; make sure to spread the crust along the entire bottom of the pan to the edges. Bake the crust for 15 minutes, then set it aside to cool. Keep the oven on.

To make the cheesecake batter, in a large bowl, add the cream cheese and cookie butter. Using an electric hand mixer on high speed, whip the ingredients in circular motions until creamy. Add in the eggs, heavy cream and vanilla, and continue to mix until the ingredients are incorporated; this should take about 5 minutes.

Wrap the outside of the cake pan in aluminum foil. Pour the cheesecake batter on top of the cooled crust. Take out a large baking pan, and fill it with about an inch (3 cm) of water. Gently place the cake pan inside the baking pan, and bake the cheesecake for 1 hour. Baking it like this will prevent the cheesecake from drying up.

When the cheesecake is done baking, remove it from the oven and let the cheesecake cool for 45 minutes at room temperature. Once the cheesecake comes to room temperature, wrap it while still in the pan with aluminum foil, and place it in the refrigerator for 8 hours.

If you choose to garnish with extra cookie butter, warm it up in a small glass container by microwaving for 30 seconds, then drizzle it on top of your cheesecake, add the cookies on top and enjoy!

INGREDIENTS

CRUST

9 oz (255 g) speculoos cookies (I prefer Biscoff cookies), finely crushed

8 tbsp (112 g) unsalted butter, melted

CHEESECAKE BATTER

24 oz (680 g) cream cheese, softened to room temperature

14 oz (392 g) cookie butter (I prefer Biscoff cookie butter)

5 eggs

1 cup (240 ml) heavy cream

1 tbsp (15 ml) vanilla extract

GARNISH (OPTIONAL)

½ cup (120 g) Biscoff cookie butter

2 speculoos cookies (I prefer Biscoff cookies)

FERRERO ROCHER® NO-BAKE CHEESECAKE

If Ferrero Rocher® is the food of the gods, then what is the Ferrero Rocher No-Bake Cheesecake? Its chocolatey cream and Ferrero Rocher candy pieces would have Zeus singing Hallelujah.

Yields 8 servings

To make the crust, in a large bowl, add the graham snacks and butter. Mix the ingredients until well combined. Place the mixture in a 9-inch (23-cm) springform cake pan; make sure to spread the crust along the entire bottom of the pan to the edges. Freeze the pan for 1 hour.

To make the cheesecake batter, in a large bowl, add the cream cheese, sugar and sour cream. Using an electric hand mixer on high speed, whip the ingredients until they're smooth and creamy. Next, add in the heavy cream, hazelnut cocoa spread, truffles and vanilla. Mix the ingredients at high speed until they are incorporated.

Pour the cheesecake batter on top of the crust. Cover the cheesecake with aluminum foil while it is still in the pan, and refrigerate it for at least 8 hours before serving.

Decorate your cheesecake by drizzling hazelnut cocoa spread on top and lining up the chocolates around the cake! Slice, serve and enjoy!

INGREDIENTS

CRUST

1 (10-oz [283-g]) box chocolate chip graham snacks (I prefer chocolate Teddy Grahams), crushed

8 tbsp (112 g) unsalted butter, melted

CHEESECAKE BATTER

24 oz (680 g) cream cheese, softened to room temperature

½ cup (100 g) white granulated sugar

¼ cup (60 ml) sour cream

1¼ cups (300 ml) heavy cream

2 tbsp (37 g) hazelnut cocoa spread (I prefer Nutella)

12 chocolate hazelnut truffles (I prefer Ferrero Rocher truffles), crushed

1 tbsp (15 ml) vanilla extract

GARNISH (OPTIONAL)

2 tbsp (37 g) hazelnut cocoa spread (I prefer Nutella)

18 chocolate hazelnut truffles (I prefer Ferrero Rocher truffles)

S'MORES CHOCOLATE CHIP CHEESECAKE

S'mores shouldn't be exclusive to the summer bonfire. They should be enjoyed year-round, especially in the shape of a creamy cheesecake. All the fun of a roasted marshmallow and none of the mosquito bites.

Yields 8 servings

Preheat the oven to 325°F (165°C). Then, take the bottom of the cake pan and evenly grease it.

To make the crust, in a large bowl, add the crackers, butter and sugar. Mix the ingredients until well combined. Place the mixture in a 9-inch (23-cm) springform cake pan; make sure to spread the crust along the entire bottom of the pan to the edges. Bake the crust for 15 minutes, then set it aside to cool. Keep the oven on.

To make the cheesecake batter, in a large bowl, add the cream cheese, sugar, vanilla and sour cream. Using an electric hand mixer on high speed, whip the ingredients in circular motions until creamy. Add in the heavy cream and eggs, and continue to mix on high speed until the ingredients are incorporated and fluffy; this should take about 5 minutes.

Next, add the cookies to the mixture and fold them in softly. Wrap the outside of the cake pan in aluminum foil. Pour the cheesecake batter on top of the cooled crust. Take out a large baking pan, and fill it with about an inch (3 cm) of water. Gently place the cake pan inside the baking pan, and bake the cheesecake for 1 hour. Baking it like this will prevent the cheesecake from drying up.

When the cheesecake is done baking, remove it from the oven and let the cheesecake cool for 1 hour at room temperature. Once the cheesecake comes to room temperature, wrap it while still in the pan with aluminum foil, and place it in the refrigerator for 8 hours. When you're ready to serve, prepare your chocolate ganache by mixing together your melted chocolate, warm heavy cream and sugar. Then, drizzle it on your cheesecake and add the marshmallow fluff and cracker.

INGREDIENTS

CRUST

8 graham crackers, finely crushed

7 tbsp (98 g) unsalted butter, melted

2 tbsp (30 g) white granulated sugar

CHEESECAKE BATTER

32 oz (896 g) cream cheese, softened to room temperature

1⅓ cups (266 g) white granulated sugar

1 tbsp (15 ml) vanilla extract

½ cup (120 ml) sour cream

½ cup (120 ml) heavy cream

6 eggs

14 chocolate chip cookies (I prefer Chips Ahoy! cookies), cut into fourths

CHOCOLATE GANACHE

3.5 oz (98 g) dark chocolate, melted

¼ cup (60 ml) warm heavy cream

1 cup (120 g) confectioners' sugar

About 1½ cups (156 g) marshmallow fluff, for topping

1 graham cracker (cut in 4)

KINDER BUENO® NO-BAKE CHEESECAKE

Behold the chocolate of your childhood in an easy no-bake cheesecake! Talk about making your dreams come true. This rich vanilla cream cheesecake with crunchy Kinder® pieces makes you feel like a kid again.

Yields 8 servings

To make the crust, in a large bowl, add the graham snacks and butter. Mix the ingredients until well combined. Place the mixture in a 9-inch (23-cm) springform cake pan; make sure to spread the crust along the entire bottom of the pan to the edges. Freeze the pan for 1 hour.

To make the cheesecake batter, in a large bowl, add the cream cheese, sugar and sour cream. Using an electric hand mixer on high speed, whip the ingredients until they're fluffy. Add in the heavy cream, wafer chocolate bars and vanilla. Mix until the ingredients are incorporated.

Pour the cheesecake batter on top of the crust. Cover the cheesecake while it is still in the pan with aluminum foil, and place it in the refrigerator for at least 8 hours. Top with hazelnut wafer chocolate bars, if using.

INGREDIENTS

CRUST

2 cups (140 g) chocolate graham snacks (I prefer Teddy Grahams), crushed

8 tbsp (112 g) unsalted butter, melted

CHEESECAKE BATTER

24 oz (680 g) cream cheese, softened to room temperature

½ cup (100 g) white granulated sugar

¼ cup (60 ml) sour cream

1¼ cups (300 ml) heavy cream

4 hazelnut wafer chocolate bars (I prefer Kinder Bueno sticks), crushed

1 tbsp (15 ml) vanilla extract

GARNISH (OPTIONAL)

Hazelnut wafer chocolate bars (I prefer Kinder Bueno sticks), cut in half

PUMPKIN PIE CHEESECAKE

This velvety Pumpkin Pie Cheesecake filled with festive spices and covered in fluffy whipped cream will forever change your invitation to Holiday parties. Do you want to accept your fate as the family dessert guru? Then jump right in.

Yields 8 servings

Preheat the oven to 325°F (165°C). Then, take the bottom of the cake pan and evenly grease it. To make the crust, in a large bowl, add the crackers and butter. Mix the ingredients until well combined. Place the mixture in a 9-inch (23-cm) springform cake pan; make sure to spread the crust along the entire bottom of the pan to the edges. Bake the crust for 12 minutes, then set it aside to cool. Keep the oven on.

To make the cheesecake batter, in a large bowl, add the cream cheese, brown sugar, granulated sugar and sour cream. Using an electric hand mixer on medium speed, whip the ingredients in circular motions until creamy. Add in the 3 eggs plus egg yolks, pumpkin, cinnamon, nutmeg, ginger and vanilla. Mix on high speed until the ingredients are incorporated. Wrap the outside of the cake pan in aluminum foil. Pour the cheesecake batter on top of the cooled crust. Take out a large baking pan, and fill it with about an inch (3 cm) of water. Gently place the cake pan inside the baking pan, and bake the cheesecake for 45 minutes. Baking it like this will prevent the cheesecake from drying up.

When the cheesecake is done baking, remove the cheesecake from the oven and let it cool to room temperature. Once the cheesecake comes to room temperature, wrap it while still in the pan with aluminum foil, and place it in the refrigerator for 6 hours.

When you're about ready to serve, make the whipped cream. In a large bowl, add the heavy cream and granulated sugar. Using an electric hand mixer on high speed, whip the ingredients until peaks form. Add a pinch of cinnamon to the mixture and mix lightly. Top the cheesecake with the whipped cream before serving.

INGREDIENTS

CRUST

16 graham crackers, pulsed into crumbs

7 tbsp (98 g) unsalted butter, melted

CHEESECAKE BATTER

24 oz (680 g) cream cheese, softened to room temperature

¾ cup (165 g) packed light brown sugar

¾ cup (150 g) white granulated sugar

½ cup (120 ml) sour cream

3 large eggs plus 2 egg yolks

1 (15-oz [425-g]) can pumpkin puree

¾ tsp cinnamon

⅛ tsp nutmeg

¼ tsp ground ginger

1½ tsp (8 ml) vanilla extract

WHIPPED CREAM

1 cup (240 ml) heavy cream

¼ cup (50 g) white granulated sugar

Pinch of cinnamon

STRAWBERRY WHITE CHOCOLATE CHEESECAKE

A classic dessert with a modern twist. This recipe takes the typical white chocolate cheesecake with a strawberry topping and makes it five times better. Combining the strawberry into the batter creates the best of both worlds.

Yields 8 servings

Preheat the oven to 325°F (165°C). Then, take the bottom of the cake pan and evenly grease it.

To make the crust, in a large bowl, add the cookies and butter. Mix the ingredients until well combined. Place the mixture in a 9-inch (23-cm) springform cake pan; make sure to spread the crust along the entire bottom of the pan to the edges. Bake the crust for 15 minutes, then set it aside to cool. Keep the oven on.

To make the cheesecake batter, in a large bowl, add the cream cheese, eggs, condensed milk, yogurt, vanilla and strawberries. Using an electric hand mixer on high speed, whip the ingredients in circular motions until creamy and smooth.

Wrap the outside of the cake pan in aluminum foil. Pour the cheesecake batter on top of the cooled crust. Take out a large baking pan, and fill it with about an inch (3 cm) of water. Gently place the cake pan inside the baking pan, and bake the cheesecake for 1 hour. Baking it like this will prevent the cheesecake from drying up.

When the cheesecake is done baking, remove the cheesecake from the oven, and let it come to room temperature. Once the cheesecake comes to room temperature, wrap the cheesecake and pan with aluminum foil, and place them in the refrigerator for 8 hours.

Before serving, top the cheesecake with white chocolate and sliced strawberries.

INGREDIENTS

CRUST

35 Spanish tea cookies (I prefer Goya Maria cookies), crushed

1½ cups (340 g) unsalted butter, melted

CHEESECAKE BATTER

24 oz (680 g) cream cheese, softened to room temperature

5 eggs

1½ (14-oz [397-g]) cans sweetened condensed milk

½ cup (120 ml) nonfat yogurt

1 tbsp (15 ml) vanilla extract

5 strawberries, hulled and blended to smoothie-like texture

TOPPINGS

8 oz (226 g) white chocolate, melted

10 strawberries, hulled and sliced in half

CHIPS AHOY!® & WHITE CHOCOLATE CHEESECAKE

If you are like me and are an avid Chips Ahoy! fan, then this one's for you! It combines all that you love about a creamy cheesecake with the twist of white chocolate and the cookie crust. Part of the cheesecake series, it's a creative take on your classic cheesecake, which will certainly be a conversation starter!

Yields 8 servings

Preheat the oven to 325°F (165°C). Then, take the bottom of the cake pan and evenly grease it.

To make the crust, in a large bowl, add the cookies and butter. Mix the ingredients until well combined. Place the mixture in a 9-inch (23-cm) springform cake pan; make sure to spread the crust along the entire bottom of the pan to the edges. Bake the crust for 15 minutes, then set it aside to cool. Keep the oven on.

To make the cheesecake batter, in a large bowl, add the cream cheese, sugar, sour cream and vanilla. Using an electric hand mixer on medium speed, whip the ingredients in circular motions until creamy. Add in the eggs and heavy cream, and mix on high speed until fluffy; this should take about 5 minutes. Fold in the white chocolate.

Wrap the outside of the cake pan in aluminum foil. Pour the cheesecake batter on top of the cooled crust. Take out a large baking pan, and fill it with about an inch (3 cm) of water. Gently place the cake pan inside the baking pan, and bake the cheesecake for 1 hour. Baking it like this will prevent the cheesecake from drying up.

When the cheesecake is done baking, remove the cheesecake from the oven, and allow it to come to room temperature for about 1 hour. Once the cheesecake comes to room temperature, wrap it with aluminum foil while it is still in the pan, and place it in the refrigerator for 8 hours.

Decorate with your whipped cream and cookies, serve and enjoy!

INGREDIENTS

CRUST

33 chocolate chip cookies (I prefer Chips Ahoy! cookies), crushed

8 tbsp (112 g) unsalted butter, melted

CHEESECAKE BATTER

32 oz (896 g) cream cheese, softened to room temperature

1⅓ cups (266 g) white granulated sugar

½ cup (120 ml) sour cream

1 tbsp (15 ml) vanilla extract

5 eggs

½ cup (120 ml) heavy cream

32 oz (896 g) white chocolate chips, melted

GARNISH (OPTIONAL)

Whipped cream (to taste)

9 chocolate chip cookies (cut in half)

CLASSIC BASQUE-STYLE CHEESECAKE

This is cheesecake 2.0—its airy, almost-souffle-like consistency makes the regular cheesecake look like the grocery-store version of this eloquent dessert. Its slightly burned exterior gives the cake a crunchy texture and a slight caramel taste.

Yields 8 servings

Preheat the oven to 400°F (205°C).

In a large bowl, add the cream cheese, sugar and vanilla. Using an electric hand mixer on medium speed, mix the ingredients until they're fluffy. Add in the eggs, heavy cream, flour and baking powder, and mix at high speed until smooth and creamy; this should take about 4 minutes.

Add a large sheet of parchment paper to an 8-inch (20-cm) cake pan; make sure the tips of the parchment paper are sticking out about 3 inches (8 cm) above the edge of the pan. (This will allow you to pull out the cheesecake after the baking is complete!)

Pour the cheesecake batter into the cake pan. Bake the cheesecake for 50 minutes. When the cheesecake is finished baking, remove it from the oven and let it cool to room temperature. Once it has come to room temperature, place the cheesecake in the refrigerator to cool overnight before serving.

INGREDIENTS

48 oz (1.4 kg) cream cheese, softened to room temperature

1 cup (200 g) white granulated sugar

1 tbsp (15 ml) vanilla extract

3 eggs

2 cups (480 ml) heavy cream

⅓ cup (40 g) cake flour

½ tsp baking powder

OREO® BASQUE-STYLE CHEESECAKE

Yes, I always find a way to include Oreos in my recipes! And you will understand why after you try this earth-shattering cheesecake. The mix between the classic Oreo flavor and fluffy cheesecake will be marked in your memories as a momentous occasion.

Yields 8 servings

INGREDIENTS

39 chocolate sandwich cookies (I prefer Oreo cookies)

48 oz (1.4 kg) cream cheese, softened to room temperature

½ cup (100 g) white granulated sugar

1 tbsp (15 ml) vanilla extract

3 eggs

2 cups (480 ml) heavy cream

⅓ cup (40 g) cake flour

½ tsp baking powder

GARNISH (OPTIONAL)

½ cup (120 ml) heavy cream

2 tbsp (16 g) confectioners' sugar

½ tsp vanilla extract

Preheat the oven to 400°F (205°C).

Pull apart each of the cookies and scrape the cookie cream into a small bowl using a butter knife. Crush the cookie pieces into fine crumbs and set aside.

In a large bowl, add the cream cheese, sugar, cookie cream and vanilla. Using an electric hand mixer on medium speed, mix the ingredients until they're fluffy. Add in the eggs, heavy cream, flour, crushed cookies and baking powder. Mix at high speed until smooth and creamy; this should take about 4 minutes.

Add a large sheet of parchment paper to an 8-inch (20-cm) cake pan; make sure the tips of the parchment paper are sticking out about 3 inches (8 cm) above the edge of the pan. (This will allow you to pull out the cheesecake after the baking is complete!)

Pour the cheesecake batter into the cake pan. Bake the cheesecake for 50 minutes. Once the cheesecake is done baking, remove it from the oven and let it cool to room temperature. Place the cheesecake in the refrigerator and cool overnight before serving.

If you decide to garnish with whipped cream, use a small bowl and electric hand mixer on high speed to whip your heavy cream, confectioners' sugar and vanilla extract until peaks form.

NUTELLA® BASQUE-STYLE CHEESECAKE

Didn't think Nutella could get any better? Think again. This Nutella Basque-Style Cheesecake highlights the unique Nutella flavor while adding a creamy and fluffy texture. It tastes like you took the poofiest cloud in the sky and dipped it in Nutella.

Yields 8 servings

Preheat the oven to 400°F (205°C).

In a large bowl, add the cream cheese, ricotta, flour and baking powder. Using an electric hand mixer on medium speed, mix the ingredients until they're creamy. Add in the eggs, heavy cream and hazelnut cocoa spread. Mix at high speed until smooth and creamy; this should take about 4 minutes.

Add a large sheet of parchment paper to an 8-inch (20-cm) cake pan; make sure the tips of the parchment paper are sticking out about 3 inches (8 cm) above the edge of the pan. (This will allow you to pull out the cheesecake after the baking is complete!)

Pour the cheesecake batter into the cake pan. Bake the cheesecake for 50 minutes. Once the cheesecake is done baking, remove it from the oven and let it cool at room temperature. Place the cheesecake in the refrigerator and cool overnight before serving.

Garnish your cheesecake with hazelnut cocoa spread and hazelnuts, serve and enjoy!

INGREDIENTS

24 oz (680 g) cream cheese, softened to room temperature

12 oz (340 g) ricotta cheese

⅓ cup (40 g) cake flour

½ tsp baking powder

3 eggs

2 cups (480 ml) heavy cream

16 tbsp (296 g) hazelnut cocoa spread (I prefer Nutella)

GARNISH (OPTIONAL)

½ cup (148 g) hazelnut cocoa spread (I prefer Nutella)

Roasted hazelnuts, chopped

DULCE DE LECHE BASQUE-STYLE CHEESECAKE

Sweeter than candy, candy of milk, this Basque-style cheesecake is more precious than silk. This cheesecake is so fine, it will make you rhyme. It has an airy texture, a crispy outer shell and the dulce de leche flavor that you will love.

Yields 8 servings

Preheat the oven to 400°F (205°C).

In a large bowl, add the cream cheese, sugar and vanilla. Using an electric hand mixer on medium speed, mix the ingredients until they're fluffy. Add in the eggs, heavy cream, flour, dulce de leche and baking powder, and mix at high speed until smooth and creamy; this should take about 4 minutes.

Add a large sheet of parchment paper to an 8-inch (20-cm) cake pan; make sure the tips of the parchment paper are sticking out about 3 inches (8 cm) above the edge of the pan. (This will allow you to pull out the cheesecake after the baking is complete!)

Pour the cheesecake batter into the cake pan. Bake the cheesecake for 50 minutes. Once the cheesecake is done baking, remove it from the oven and let it cool at room temperature. Place the cheesecake in the refrigerator and cool overnight before serving.

Garnish with extra dulce de leche by pouring on top and piping around the edges, serve and enjoy!

INGREDIENTS

36 oz (1 kg) cream cheese, softened to room temperature

1 cup (220 g) packed light brown sugar

1 tbsp (15 ml) vanilla extract

3 eggs

2 cups (480 ml) heavy cream

⅓ cup (40 g) cake flour

16 oz (454 g) dulce de leche

½ tsp baking powder

GARNISH (OPTIONAL)

8 oz (225 g) dulce de leche

BISCOFF® COOKIES BASQUE-STYLE CHEESECAKE

With Basque cheesecake's European origins, it's only right to create
a flavor using a European staple—Biscoff cookies! This cookie's
deep caramel flavor perfectly complements the creaminess of the
cheesecake. Not to mention it's topped with vanilla pudding.
This one gets straight "Wows!" across the board.

Yields 8 servings

Preheat the oven to 400°F (205°C).

In a large bowl, add the cream cheese, sugar, cookie butter and
vanilla. Using an electric hand mixer on medium speed, mix
the ingredients until they're fluffy. Add in the eggs, heavy
cream, flour and baking powder, and mix at high speed until
smooth and creamy; this should take about 4 minutes.

Add a large sheet of parchment paper to an 8-inch (20-cm)
cake pan; make sure the tips of the parchment paper are
sticking out about 3 inches (8 cm) above the edge of the pan.
(This will allow you to pull out the cheesecake after the baking
is complete!)

Pour the cheesecake batter into the cake pan. Bake the
cheesecake for 50 minutes. Once the cheesecake is done
baking, remove it from the oven and let it cool to room
temperature. Place the cheesecake in the refrigerator and cool
overnight before serving.

Before serving, top with cookies and pudding.

INGREDIENTS

32 oz (896 g) cream cheese, softened to room temperature

1 cup (220 g) packed light brown sugar

1 (14-oz [396-g]) jar cookie butter (I prefer Biscoff cookie butter)

1 tbsp (15 ml) vanilla extract

3 eggs

2 cups (480 ml) heavy cream

⅓ cup (40 g) cake flour

½ tsp baking powder

5 speculoos cookies (I prefer Biscoff cookies), crumbled

1 cup (280 g) vanilla pudding

GUAVA & COOKIES BASQUE-STYLE CHEESECAKE

Coming from Colombian heritage, guava has a special place in my heart. Especially guava and cheese as a pair! Their sweet-and-salty relationship is so iconic, it deserves a cheesecake. The cake base is made with guava paste and topped with syrupy vanilla pudding. It's absolutely delicious!

Yields 8 servings

Preheat the oven to 400°F (205°C).

In a large bowl, add the cream cheese, sugar, guava paste and vanilla. Using an electric hand mixer on medium speed, mix the ingredients until they're fluffy and creamy. Add in the eggs, heavy cream, flour and baking powder, and mix at high speed until smooth and creamy; this should take about 4 minutes.

Add a large sheet of parchment paper to an 8-inch (20-cm) cake pan; make sure the tips of the parchment paper are sticking out about 3 inches (8 cm) above the edge of the pan. (This will allow you to pull out the cheesecake after the baking is complete!)

Pour the cheesecake batter into the cake pan. Bake the cheesecake for 45 minutes. The cheesecake will be jiggly when you take it out. Let it cool at room temperature for 1 hour. Place the cheesecake in the refrigerator and cool for at least 6 hours.

Just before serving, top the cheesecake with the pudding. If you want to make the pudding runnier and syrupier, whisk it with small amounts of milk until it reaches the desired consistency. Then top the cheesecake with crumbled cookies and guava bits.

INGREDIENTS

32 oz (896 g) cream cheese, softened to room temperature

1 cup (200 g) white granulated sugar

1 (14-oz [392-g]) pack guava paste

1 tbsp (15 ml) vanilla extract

3 eggs

2 cups (480 ml) heavy cream

⅓ cup (40 g) cake flour

½ tsp baking powder

1 cup (280 g) vanilla pudding

1 cup (240 ml) milk, optional

7 Spanish tea cookies (I prefer Goya Maria cookies), crumbled

Cubed guava paste, for topping

TIRAMISU BASQUE-STYLE CHEESECAKE

This is an easy way to spice up your go-to tiramisu dessert. This will take you from a simple layered ladyfinger tower to a complex creation. The smooth texture of the tiramisu cream and the crunchy exterior of the cheesecake will leave you and your family wanting more.

Yields 8 servings

Preheat the oven to 400°F (205°C).

In a large bowl, add the cream cheese, sugar and vanilla. Using an electric hand mixer on medium speed, mix the ingredients until they're fluffy. Add in the eggs, heavy cream, flour, baking powder and coffee, and mix at high speed until smooth and creamy; this should take about 4 minutes.

Add a large sheet of parchment paper to an 8-inch (20-cm) cake pan; make sure the tips of the parchment paper are sticking out about 3 inches (8 cm) above the edge of the pan. (This will allow you to pull out the cheesecake after the baking is complete!)

Pour the cheesecake batter into the cake pan. Bake the cheesecake for 50 minutes. When the cheesecake is done baking, remove it from the oven and let it cool to room temperature. Place the cheesecake in the refrigerator and cool overnight before serving.

Before serving, you'll make the tiramisu topping. In a large bowl, add the heavy cream, mascarpone, vanilla and sugar. Using an electric hand mixer on medium speed, mix the ingredients until they're fluffy and creamy. Set the cream mixture aside.

Take out the cheesecake from the refrigerator. Place ladyfingers on the top of the cheesecake, covering the surface completely. Carefully pour the espresso over the ladyfingers, drenching them completely. Layer the cream mixture on top of the ladyfingers, and dust the top with cocoa powder. Serve immediately.

INGREDIENTS

32 oz (896 g) cream cheese, softened to room temperature

1 cup (200 g) white granulated sugar

1 tbsp (15 ml) vanilla extract

3 eggs

2 cups (480 ml) heavy cream

⅓ cup (40 g) cake flour

½ tsp baking powder

1 cup (240 ml) cold brew coffee

TIRAMISU TOPPING

1 cup (240 ml) heavy cream

6 oz (170 g) mascarpone cheese

3 tbsp (45 ml) vanilla extract

½ cup (100 g) white granulated sugar

48 ladyfingers cookies

2 (1-oz [30-ml]) espresso shots, cold

5 tbsp (25 g) unsweetened cocoa powder

KINDER BUENO®
BASQUE-STYLE CHEESECAKE

If you think the crisp wafer and silky hazelnut filling in a Kinder Bueno hits different, then the smooth, creamy Kinder Bueno center and slightly caramelized shell of this cheesecake will send you into another dimension . . . or maybe an alternate universe.

Yields 8 servings

Preheat the oven to 400°F (205°C).

In a large bowl, add the cream cheese, sugar and vanilla. Using an electric hand mixer on medium speed, mix the ingredients until they're fluffy.

To make the cookie paste: In a blender, add the hazelnut chocolate bars and 1 cup (240 ml) of heavy cream. Blend until smooth.

Add in the hazelnut chocolate bar paste, remaining heavy cream, eggs, flour and baking powder into the cream cheese mixture. Mix at high speed until smooth and creamy.

Add a large sheet of parchment paper to an 8-inch (20-cm) cake pan; make sure the tips of the parchment paper are sticking out about 3 inches (8 cm) above the edge of the pan. (This will allow you to pull out the cheesecake after the baking is complete!)

Pour the cheesecake batter into the cake pan. Bake the cheesecake for 50 minutes. Once the cheesecake is done baking, remove it from the oven and let it cool to room temperature. Place the cheesecake in the refrigerator and cool overnight.

If adding garnish, cover with hazelnut cocoa spread and hazelnut wafer chocolate bars before serving. Slice and enjoy!

INGREDIENTS

32 oz (896 g) cream cheese, softened to room temperature

1 cup (200 g) white granulated sugar

1 tbsp (15 ml) vanilla extract

10 hazelnut wafer chocolate bars (I prefer Kinder Bueno sticks)

2 cups (480 ml) heavy cream, divided

3 eggs

⅓ cup (40 g) cake flour

½ tsp baking powder

GARNISH (OPTIONAL)

3 tbsp (56 g) hazelnut cocoa spread (I prefer Nutella)

Hazelnut wafer chocolate bars (I prefer Kinder Bueno sticks), cut in half

PIES FOR
All Seasons

No, pie isn't just for the holidays. Pie's creamy and crispy deliciousness can be enjoyed all year round—both solo and with your loved ones! In this chapter, you can find my top five favorite pies for any occasion. Birthday: flan pie (page 102). Retirement party: Fudge Brownie Pie (page 97). Divorce party: already-over-him apple pie (page 94). You heard it here first: pie is the new cake.

EVERYONE'S FAVORITE APPLE PIE

This dessert simply never goes out of style! Its buttery pie crust and cinnamon apple filling offers a heartwarming experience. Some might even say "love at first bite."

Yields 6 servings

Preheat the oven to 375°F (190°C).

Line a 9-inch (23-cm) pie pan with the pie pastry, and trim the edges to fit. Bake using pie weights in the center for about 10 minutes, then let cool completely.

In a large bowl, mix the apples with lemon juice, butter, cinnamon, ginger, nutmeg, cornstarch, zest and both sugars. Refrigerate for 3 hours to let the juices settle.

Pour the apple mix (without the juices) into the prepared pie pastry, and seal the pie with the remaining pastry. Pinch the edges to connect.

Bake the pie for 45 minutes. Let it cool for 3 to 4 hours before serving.

INGREDIENTS

2 pre-made pie crusts

44 oz (1.3 kg) apples, sliced and peeled, about 12 apples (works best with 4 each of honeycrisp, gala and Granny Smith)

1 tbsp (15 ml) lemon juice

2 tbsp (28 g) unsalted butter, melted

1 tsp cinnamon

1 tsp ground ginger

½ tsp nutmeg

2 tbsp (16 g) cornstarch

1 tsp lemon zest

½ cup (100 g) white granulated sugar

¾ cup (165 g) packed light brown sugar

FUDGE BROWNIE PIE

Bake the world a better place with this Fudge Brownie Pie! It's crunchy on the outside and fudgy in the middle. Forget brookies—those are yesterday's news! The future is the piownie (pie + brownie)!

Yields 6 servings

Preheat the oven to 350°F (180°C).

Line a 9-inch (23-cm) pie pan with the pie crust, and trim the edges to fit. Bake using pie weights in the center for about 10 minutes, then let cool completely.

In a large bowl, add the chocolates, butter, flour, eggs, sugar, vanilla and cocoa powder. Using an electric hand mixer on high speed, mix the ingredients until well combined.

Pour the ingredients into the prepared pie crust and bake for 25 minutes. Remove the pie from the oven, and cover the edges of the pie crust with foil to protect from burning. Bake for an additional 40 minutes. Let the pie cool completely before serving.

INGREDIENTS

1 pre-made pie crust

3 oz (85 g) unsweetened chocolate, melted

2 oz (57 g) semisweet chocolate, melted

8 tbsp (112 g) unsalted butter, melted

1 cup (125 g) all-purpose flour

3 eggs

2 cups (400 g) white granulated sugar

1 tbsp (15 ml) vanilla extract

⅓ cup (32 g) unsweetened cocoa powder

OREO® BISCOFF® PIE

I never thought the day would come . . . I have created a dessert with my two favorite cookies! This recipe includes the classic chocolatey taste of the Oreo and the deep spice flavor of the Biscoff. I can die a happy man, and you will feel the same after you try this pie.

Yields 6 servings

Preheat the oven to 350°F (180°C).

To make the crust, in a large bowl, add the cookies and butter. Mix the ingredients until well combined. Place the mixture into a pie pan and spread it out evenly. Make sure to spread the crust along the entire bottom and along the edges of the pan. Bake the crust for 13 minutes, then set it aside to cool.

To make the filling, in a large bowl, add the cream cheese, sugar and cookie butter. Using an electric hand mixer on high speed, mix the ingredients until they're well combined. Add the sour cream and heavy cream, and mix until they're incorporated.

Pour the filling into the cooled pie shell, and refrigerate it for 3 hours. Top with the crushed cookies, if using.

INGREDIENTS

CRUST

27 chocolate sandwich cookies (I prefer Oreo cookies), finely crushed

6 tbsp (84 g) unsalted butter, melted

FILLING

8 oz (226 g) cream cheese, softened

½ cup (60 g) confectioners' sugar

1 (14-oz [396-g]) jar cookie butter (I prefer Biscoff cookie butter)

1 cup (240 ml) sour cream

½ cup (120 ml) heavy cream

TOPPINGS (OPTIONAL)

Chocolate sandwich cookies (I prefer Oreo cookies), crushed

Speculoos cookies (I prefer Biscoff cookies), crushed

CREAMY TIRAMISU PIE

Bored of eating the same old tiramisu? Turn it into a pie! This recipe is composed of a flaky pie crust, layers of velvety cream and ladyfingers soaked in cold brew coffee. Eating this dessert will have you occu-pied.

Yields 6 servings

Preheat the oven to 375°F (190°C).

Stretch the pie crust across a 9-inch (23-cm) pie pan, gently folding in the corners, and coat the crust with butter and 1 tablespoon (15 g) sugar. Bake using pie weights in the center for about 10 minutes, then let cool completely.

To make the filling, in a large bowl, whip the heavy cream, remaining sugar, vanilla and mascarpone until peaks form. In a small bowl, add the espresso and dip each ladyfinger into it quickly. Place a layer of the soaked cookies in the cooled pie crust. Dollop the cream mixture on top of the ladyfingers. Continue to layer the cookies and cream until you've used all the prepared ingredients.

Refrigerate the pie for 3 hours. Just before serving, dust the top of the pie with cocoa powder and top with extra ladyfinger cookies.

INGREDIENTS

1 pre-made pie crust

1 tbsp (14 g) unsalted butter, melted

½ cup (100 g) plus 1 tbsp (15 g) white granulated sugar, divided

2 cups (480 ml) heavy cream

3 tbsp (45 ml) vanilla extract

8 oz (226 g) mascarpone cheese

1½ cups (360 ml) espresso, cold

15 ladyfinger cookies, plus more for garnish

5 tbsp (25 g) unsweetened cocoa powder

EASY FLAN PIE

A pie that keeps it classy! This crispy pie crust is filled with a rich vanilla filling and topped with silky dulce de leche. Its simplicity and diverse flavors will keep you coming back for more.

Yields 6 servings

Preheat the oven to 375°F (190°C).

Stretch the pie crust across a 9-inch (23-cm) pie pan, gently folding in the corners. Bake using pie weights in the center for about 13 minutes, then let cool completely.

In a large bowl, add the eggs, condensed milk, milk, sugar and vanilla. Using an electric hand mixer on high speed, mix the ingredients until well combined. Pour the filling into the crust.

Bake the pie for 15 minutes. After 15 minutes, reduce the heat to 350°F (180°C), and bake for an additional 15 minutes. Let the pie cool, then add the dulce de leche before serving (if using).

INGREDIENTS

1 pre-made pie crust

4 eggs

1 (14-oz [397-g]) can sweetened condensed milk

1 cup (240 ml) milk

½ cup (100 g) white granulated sugar

1 tsp vanilla extract

7 oz (198 g) dulce de leche, for topping (optional)

Quick

(BUT IMPRESSIVE)
LAST-MINUTE
TREATS

If you're like me, then you always attempt to make the best possible impression. Especially when it comes to food. However, sometimes there is not enough time to create extravagant desserts, and the store-bought ones are just not going to cut it. This is when this chapter comes in handy—it introduces fun and easy ways to make delicious desserts, including various recipes you can choose from to accommodate whoever you are hosting. Is your aunt who eats gluten-free coming over? Try making the Flourless Chocolate Cake (page 117). Are your younger cousins tagging along? How do they feel about Banana S'mores Pop-Tarts® (page 106)? These simple treats will make your friends and family feel loved all while making you look like a baking god.

BANANA S'MORES POP-TARTS®

Homemade Pop-Tarts are always a good idea! Especially if they have chocolate and bananas. This flakey pastry with marshmallow fluff is what some would call a succulent bite.

Yields 2 servings

Preheat the oven to 400°F (205°C).

Unroll the pie crusts on a clean surface. Using a knife, carefully slice the rounded sides from each side of the pie crusts, creating two even rectangles. Slice the pie crusts into 3 x 2–inch (8 x 5–cm) rectangles. In the middle of two rectangles, place 3 squares of milk chocolate and 2 slices of banana. Place the other rectangles on top of the first rectangles, and pinch the edges closed using your hands or a fork.

Place the tarts on a baking sheet.

To make the egg wash, in a small bowl, add the egg and buttermilk, and whisk them together. Spread the egg wash over each pop tart and bake for 20 minutes.

Once the tarts are done baking, top them with marshmallow fluff and cracker crumbs. Serve immediately.

PRO TIP: *You can use a kitchen torch to lightly brown the marshmallow fluff!*

INGREDIENTS

1 (14-oz [397-g]) box pie crust (two crusts)

5 oz (142 g) milk chocolate, cut into squares

½ banana

1 egg, beaten

1 tsp buttermilk

2 tbsp (13 g) marshmallow fluff, for topping

1 graham cracker, crumbled

SIX-INGREDIENT CINNAMON ROLLS

So simple, yet so scrumptious! With only six ingredients, a world of flavor is unleashed. These homemade rolls will make the bakeries' rolls taste like amateur work. You can also add a scoop of ice cream when serving! (Check out my guides tab on Instagram @succulentbite; I have a bunch of easy flavors to make at home!) You can also add icing to your rolls for an extra sweet and sticky touch!

Yields 5 servings

Preheat the oven to 350°F (180°C).

Line a 9-inch (23-cm) springform cake pan with parchment paper and set aside.

Place a sheet of parchment paper down on the counter. Roll out the dough, and sprinkle it evenly with the brown sugar, chocolate, banana and cinnamon. Next, sprinkle the butter over the pastry and filling.

Roll the dough up from one end to the other. Slice the dough into 2- to 3-inch (5- to 8-cm)-thick pieces, and place the rolls swirl-side up in the prepared pan. Bake for about 15 minutes, or until the dough looks golden and fluffy. Remove the rolls from the oven, and let them cool slightly before serving.

INGREDIENTS

1 (8-oz [226-g]) tube crescent dough

½ cup (110 g) packed light brown sugar

2 oz (57 g) dark chocolate, shaved

½ banana, sliced

¼ cup (31 g) cinnamon

4 tbsp (56 g) unsalted butter, shaved

DATE NIGHT BOOZY BROWNIES

How many brownies do you think you need to eat to get a buzz?
Eating while trying to get tipsy might seem counteractive, but it's a
great excuse to eat two pans of these fluffy liqueur-spiked brownies.

Yields 6 servings

Preheat the oven to 350°F (180°C).

Grease an 8-inch (20-cm) brownie pan.

In a large bowl, add the caramel liqueur, butter, oil, eggs, cocoa powder, flour, baking powder, sugar and vanilla. Whisk the ingredients until they are well combined.

Pour the batter into the prepared pan. Bake the brownies for 25 minutes, and let them cool at room temperature. Once they've cooled slightly, slice and serve with a scoop of ice cream and a drizzle of chocolate liqueur.

INGREDIENTS

⅓ cup (80 ml) caramel liqueur (I prefer Chopin Dorda Sea Salt Caramel liqueur)

4 tbsp (56 g) unsalted butter, melted

¼ cup (60 ml) vegetable oil

2 eggs

1½ tbsp (8 g) unsweetened cocoa powder

1½ cups (188 g) all-purpose flour

1 tsp baking powder

1½ cups (300 g) white granulated sugar

1 tsp vanilla extract

¼ cup (40 g) vanilla ice cream, for topping

Chocolate liqueur (I prefer Chopin Dorda Double Chocolate liqueur), for topping

EASY BANANA BREAD

A good banana bread can cure anything. Sad, eat banana bread. Hungry, eat banana bread. Bought too many bananas, make banana bread. Only have bananas, make banana bread. Wife's hangry, make banana bread. All I'm saying is, this bread has powers.

Yields 6 servings

Preheat the oven to 350°F (180°C).

Grease a bread loaf pan and set aside.

In a large bowl, add the butter and sugar. Using an electric hand mixer on high speed, mix the ingredients until they're well combined.

Add the bananas, baking powder, eggs, vanilla, walnuts and flour to the bowl, and mix until incorporated.

Pour the batter into the prepared pan and bake for 50 minutes, or when an inserted toothpick comes out clean. Let the bread cool slightly before serving.

INGREDIENTS

8 tbsp (112 g) unsalted butter, softened

8 tbsp (112 g) unsalted butter, melted

4 very ripe bananas

2 tsp (9 g) baking powder

2 eggs

2 tsp (10 ml) vanilla extract

1 cup (120 g) chopped walnuts

1½ cups (188 g) all-purpose flour

PRESSURE-COOKER BROWNIES

Pressure Cooker Brownies hit different . . . they're spongier,
have a slight crisp and are really fun to make. Instead of watching
the brownies in the oven, you watch as the steam from the
pot rises. I don't know about you, but that's pretty cool . . .
or should I say steamy?

Yields 6 servings

Grease a 6-inch (15-cm) cake pan.

In a large bowl, add the butter, sugar, cocoa powder, vanilla, flour, chocolate, eggs and baking powder. Using an electric hand mixer on high speed, mix the ingredients until they're well combined.

Pour the batter into the prepared pan, and place the pan into a pressure cooker. Cook the brownies for 12 minutes at 390°F (200°C) (or on high heat). If you'd like to use the oven instead, bake the brownies at 350°F (180°C) for about 25 minutes. Once cooked, let them cool before serving.

INGREDIENTS

7 tbsp (98 g) unsalted butter

1¼ cups (250 g) white granulated sugar

⅓ cup (32 g) unsweetened cocoa powder

1 tbsp (15 ml) vanilla extract

1 cup (125 g) all-purpose flour

4 oz (113 g) dark chocolate, shaved

2 eggs

1 tsp baking powder

FLOURLESS CHOCOLATE CAKE

Don't be fooled, "flour-less" doesn't mean this cake is any "less." If anything, its absence of flour allows for the cake to be packed with more of its decadent chocolate flavor. Think of it like the absence of a social life in high school making you a more interesting person.

Yields 6 servings

Preheat the oven to 350°F (180°C). Line an 8-inch (20-cm) pan with a circle of parchment paper, then grease the exposed sides of the pan.

In a small saucepan over low heat, melt the butter and dark chocolate. Then, mix until well combined.

In a large bowl, add the sugar, eggs, vanilla and cocoa powder. Mix them together, then add the chocolate-butter mixture.

Pour the batter into the prepared pan and set aside. Take out a large baking pan, and fill it with about an inch (3 cm) of water. Gently place the cake pan inside the baking pan, and bake the cake for 30 minutes. Remove the cake from the oven, let cool for about 1 hour at room temperature and then refrigerate uncovered for 4 hours.

Before serving, prepare the ganache. In a medium-sized bowl, add the chocolate and heavy cream. Gently mix the ingredients together until they're well combined. Spoon the ganache onto the top of the cake, add the chocolate shavings, if using, serve and enjoy!

INGREDIENTS

CAKE

8 tbsp (112 g) unsalted butter

7 oz (198 g) dark chocolate, finely chopped

1 cup (200 g) white granulated sugar

4 eggs

1 tbsp (15 ml) vanilla extract

¼ cup (22 g) unsweetened cocoa powder

GANACHE

5 oz (142 g) dark chocolate, melted

⅔ cup (160 ml) heavy cream

GARNISH (OPTIONAL)

4 oz (113 g) dark chocolate, shaved

OREO® WHIPPED COFFEE SHAKE

This is the caffeinated version of the Oreo shake you used to order at a diner. It's not only going to throw you back, but it'll whip you out of your midday haze. It's creamy, sweet and provides a tasty energy boost.

Yields 2 servings

In a blender, add the coffee, heavy cream, cookies, condensed milk, ice and cocoa powder. Blend the ingredients until they are very creamy.

Serve the shake in the desired cup and top it with whipped cream.

INGREDIENTS

1 scant cup (240 ml) coffee, ice cold

1 cup (240 ml) heavy cream, cold

6 chocolate sandwich cookies (I prefer Oreo cookies)

⅓ cup (80 ml) sweetened condensed milk

5 ice cubes

1 tsp unsweetened cocoa powder

Whipped cream, for topping

CHOCOLATE SPICE BROWNIES

In this recipe, you take the already-sweet, gooey, mouthwatering brownie and you make it interesting. The addition of cinnamon, ginger and allspice is sure to be a yummy surprise. Cue the TikTok sound—"add a little bit of spice."

Yields 10 servings

Preheat the oven to 350°F (180°C).

Line an 8-inch (20-cm) baking pan with parchment paper.

In a small saucepan over low heat, melt the chocolate and butter, and stir until smooth.

In a large bowl, add the chocolate-butter mixture, flour, cinnamon, ginger, allspice, syrup, sugars and eggs. Using an electric hand mixer, mix the ingredients at low speed until they're well combined.

Pour the batter into the prepared pan, and spread it evenly. Bake for 30 minutes, then let it cool for about 1 hour before serving.

INGREDIENTS

10 oz (283 g) 60% cacao bittersweet chocolate

8 tbsp (112 g) unsalted butter

1 cup (125 g) all-purpose flour

½ tsp cinnamon

½ tsp ground ginger

½ tsp allspice

¼ cup (60 ml) maple syrup

½ cup (110 g) packed light brown sugar

½ cup (100 g) white granulated sugar

3 eggs

TRES LECHES CAKE

A cake with three milks is a cake three times as good. This spongy cake absorbs the sweet milk to create a moist, soft dessert. It's like dipping your favorite cookie in milk . . . but way better. It's topped with silky whipped cream and cinnamon. What's not to love?

Yields 10 servings

Preheat the oven to 375°F (190°C).

Grease a 9 x 13–inch (23 x 33–cm) cake pan and set aside.

To make the cake, in a large bowl, add the butter and granulated sugar. Using an electric hand mixer, mix the ingredients until they're fluffy.

Add the confectioners' sugar, flour, baking powder, baking soda, vanilla and eggs to the butter mixture. Mix the ingredients until they're incorporated.

Pour the batter into the prepared pan. Bake the cake for 20 minutes; make sure you pay attention to timing, as vigilance is vital to get just the right dryness. The cake has to be dry enough to properly absorb the milks that will be added later. Once it is finished baking, remove the cake from the oven and let it cool for 1 hour. Pierce the top of the cake evenly with a fork; there should be 1 stab every ½ inch (1 cm) on the cake top.

To make the milk bath, in a medium-sized bowl, add all the milks and mix them together. Pour the milk mixture over the top of the cake.

To make the whipped cream, in a large bowl, add the heavy cream, sugar and cinnamon. Using an electric hand mixer on high speed, mix the ingredients until they're creamy and fluffy.

Spread the whipped cream evenly across the cake's surface. Refrigerate overnight before serving.

INGREDIENTS

CAKE

8 tbsp (112 g) unsalted butter

¾ cup (150 g) white granulated sugar

¼ cup (30 g) confectioners' sugar

1½ cups (188 g) all-purpose flour

½ tsp baking powder

½ tsp baking soda

1 tsp vanilla extract

4 eggs

MILK BATH

2 cups (480 ml) whole milk

1 (14-oz [397-g]) can sweetened condensed milk

1 (12-oz [354-ml]) can evaporated milk

WHIPPED CREAM

3 cups (720 ml) heavy cream

½ cup (60 g) confectioners' sugar

Cinnamon (to taste)

KINDER® CHOCOLATE LATTE

Make your mornings more exciting with this fun coffee creation. Its sweet chocolate and creamy ice cream will give you the boost necessary to take on the day with a smile. Big-chain coffee houses have nothing on this Kinder Chocolate Latte. Not to mention it looks super cool in pictures.

Yields 1 serving

Start by opening the chocolate egg, and then carefully filling it with ice cream. Dust the ice cream with cocoa powder, then gently close the egg at the opening. Place the egg on a plate, and freeze it for 15 minutes.

Carefully place the frozen egg at the bottom of a coffee mug. Pour the hot prepared espresso shot into the mug, over the egg.

Gently pour in the hot milk, and enjoy immediately.

INGREDIENTS

1 Kinder egg

¼ cup (40 g) vanilla ice cream

1 tsp unsweetened cocoa powder

1 (1-oz [30-ml]) espresso shot, hot

⅓ cup (80 ml) milk, hot

HOMEMADE NUTELLA®

Nutella may be good, but homemade Nutella is something else. Its silky texture and roasted hazelnut flavor will drive you nuts. Some may even argue it's healthy! So, if it's good for your health, then one more spoonful is only necessary.

Yields about 5 servings

In the bowl of a food processor, add the hazelnuts and blend them until they are well combined and creamy. You'll have to stop the food processor and scrape the sides with a spatula a few times to make sure all the pieces are blended well.

Add the cocoa powder, sugar and chocolates to the food processor while continuing to blend. Once incorporated, carefully add the oil and blend until smooth and combined. Store in a glass container with a lid in the refrigerator for up to 1 week.

INGREDIENTS

1 cup (130 g) roasted and blanched hazelnuts (I purchase them already blanched from my local supermarket)

⅓ cup (32 g) unsweetened cocoa powder

1 cup (120 g) confectioners' sugar

3 oz (85 g) dark chocolate, melted

3 oz (85 g) milk chocolate, melted

3 tbsp (45 ml) avocado oil or vegetable oil

HOMEMADE WHITE CHOCOLATE NUTELLA®

This Homemade White Chocolate Nutella is like the regular Nutella's hotter sister. She's a little crazy and lacks refinement but who cares? If you've ever had the privilege of trying white chocolate Nutella, just know this one is better.

Yields about 5 servings

In the bowl of a food processor, add the hazelnuts and blend them until they are well combined and creamy. You'll have to stop the food processor and scrape the sides with a spatula a few times to make sure all the pieces are blended well.

Add the white chocolate, sugar and vanilla to the food processor while continuing to blend. Once incorporated, carefully add the oil and blend until smooth and combined. Store in a glass container with a lid in the refrigerator for up to 1 week.

INGREDIENTS

1 cup (130 g) roasted and blanched hazelnuts

6 oz (170 g) white chocolate, melted

1 cup (120 g) confectioners' sugar

1 tbsp (15 ml) vanilla extract

5 tbsp (75 ml) vegetable oil or avocado oil

EASY ALMOND BUTTER

If you've tried almond butter, you know how much of a pantry essential it is. It's tasty on toast, in smoothies, with fruit or just on a large spoon . . . with a small pack of almonds, you can create endless possibilities of yummy snacks. Beware: this silky paste may become your new obsession.

Yields about 5 servings

Preheat the oven to 350°F (180°C).

Spread the almonds on a baking sheet, and bake them for 10 minutes. Once done, let the almonds cool briefly.

Add the cooled almonds to the bowl of a food processor and blend them until they are well combined and creamy. You'll have to stop the food processor and scrape the sides with a spatula a few times to make sure all the pieces are blended well.

Once the almonds are almost creamy, add oil and salt. Keep blending until the ingredients are well combined and the butter is smooth. Store in a glass container with a lid in the refrigerator for up to 1 week.

INGREDIENTS

2 cups (286 g) almonds

1 tsp avocado oil

1 tsp salt

Must-Make
CRÊPES AND MUG CAKES

I consider crêpes to be one of the best creations known to humankind. They're thin, crispy, sweet and can be filled with literally anything. Ham and cheese? Yes! Oreos? Yes! Sautéed duck? Yes! Anything you can think of is instantly made better when paired with a crêpe.

I could say the same about mug cakes! They take the glory of a cake and put it into a personal portion. No overeating, no food waste and no sharing. We have Bill Gates to thank for Microsoft®, Mark Zuckerberg for Facebook®, a French woman who spilled porridge for the crêpe and a YouTube user who was trying a neighbor's recipe for the mug cake. Where would society be without these four innovators?

NESQUIK® OREO® CRÊPE

Looking to satisfy your crêpe craving? Well, look no further, this Nesquik Oreo Crêpe is packed with some of the best chocolatey snacks. Its batter has Oreo pieces and is filled with silky chocolate chips. This recipe is sure to leave you smiling.

Yields 1 crêpe

In a large bowl, add the eggs, milk, water, butter, chocolate milk powder and flour. Using an electric hand mixer, mix the ingredients until they're well combined.

In a large skillet on medium heat, scatter the cookies. Pour the batter over the bed of cookies, and let it cook for about 1½ minutes, then carefully flip the crêpe over and cook for the same amount of time on the other side. (This crêpe is thicker than usual, in order for the batter to hold the cookie crumbs inside!)

Add the chocolate chips to the middle of the crêpe, and fold it over twice in the pan, making a thick triangle. Put the crêpe on a plate, and add Nutella, a scoop of ice cream and extra Oreos!

INGREDIENTS

2 eggs

½ cup (120 ml) milk

½ cup (120 ml) water

2 tbsp (28 g) unsalted butter, melted

2 tbsp (14 g) chocolate milk powder (I prefer chocolate Nesquik)

1 cup (125 g) all-purpose flour

5 chocolate sandwich cookies (I prefer Oreo cookies), crushed, plus more for topping

⅓ cup (55 g) dark and white chocolate chips, mixed

½ cup (148 g) hazelnut cocoa spread (I prefer Nutella)

½ cup (80 g) vanilla ice cream, for serving

CHIPS AHOY!® CRÊPE

This isn't any ordinary crêpe; this crêpe's batter is infused with crunchy cookie pieces and sweet strawberry Nesquik. Its golden body is filled with white chocolate and topped with creamy Nutella. Do your taste buds a favor and try this out.

Yields 1 crêpe

In a large bowl, add the eggs, milk, water, butter and flour. Using an electric hand mixer, mix the ingredients until they're well combined. Add in the strawberry milk powder and mix until it's well incorporated.

In a large skillet on medium heat, scatter the cookies. Pour the batter over the bed of cookies, and let it cook for about 1½ minutes, then carefully flip the crêpe over and cook for the same amount of time on the other side. (This crêpe is thicker than usual, in order for the batter to hold the cookie crumbs inside!)

Add the chocolate chips to the middle of the crêpe, and fold it over twice in the pan, making a thick triangle. Put the crêpe on a plate, and add hazelnut cocoa spread, a scoop of ice cream and extra cookies!

INGREDIENTS

2 eggs

½ cup (120 ml) milk

½ cup (120 ml) water

2 tbsp (28 g) unsalted butter, melted

1 cup (125 g) all-purpose flour

3 tbsp (21 g) strawberry milk powder (I prefer strawberry Nesquik)

5 chocolate chip cookies (I prefer Chips Ahoy! cookies), crushed, plus more for topping

½ cup (84 g) white chocolate chips

⅓ cup (99 g) hazelnut cocoa spread (I prefer Nutella)

½ cup (80 g) vanilla ice cream

S'MORES FLUFF CRÊPE

S'mores but the French way? This recipe is everything you love
about the classic campfire treat but encased in a crispy thin pancake.
Its graham cracker batter and fluffy marshmallow filling
will have you saying, "Oui, oui!"

Yields 1 crêpe

In a large bowl, add the eggs, milk, water, butter and flour.
Using an electric hand mixer, mix the ingredients until they're
well combined.

In a large skillet on medium heat, scatter the crackers. Pour
the batter over the bed of crackers, and let it cook for about
1½ minutes, then carefully flip the crêpe over and cook for
the same amount of time on the other side. (This crêpe is
thicker than usual, in order for the batter to hold the cracker
crumbs inside!)

Add the chocolate to one half of the crêpe, then add the
marshmallow fluff to the other half. Fold it over twice in
the pan, making a thick triangle. Put the crêpe on a plate, and
serve it with ice cream.

INGREDIENTS

2 eggs

½ cup (120 ml) milk

½ cup (120 ml) water

2 tbsp (28 g) unsalted butter,
melted

1 cup (125 g) all-purpose flour

3 graham crackers, crushed

2 oz (57 g) milk chocolate

4 tbsp (26 g) marshmallow fluff

½ cup (80 g) vanilla ice cream

OREO® CHOCOLATE CHIP CRÊPE

A flavor that makes you want to celebrate the joys of life. This delicate Nutella crêpe is filled with dark chocolate chips and pieces of everyone's favorite cookie sandwich—Oreos! It's topped with creamy vanilla ice cream and a Nutella drizzle. This definitely calls for a celebration.

Yields 1 crêpe

In a large bowl, add the eggs, flour, butter, milk, hazelnut cocoa spread and water. Using an electric hand mixer, mix the ingredients until they're well combined.

In a large skillet on medium heat, pour in the batter, and let it cook for about 1½ minutes, then carefully flip the crêpe over and cook for the same amount of time on the other side. (This crêpe is thicker than usual, in order for the batter to hold the cookie crumbs inside!)

Add both chocolate chips to one side of the crêpe, and add the cookies to the other side. Fold it over twice in the pan, making a thick triangle. Put the crêpe on a plate, and serve with ice cream.

INGREDIENTS

2 eggs

1 cup (125 g) all-purpose flour

2 tbsp (28 g) unsalted butter, melted

½ cup (120 ml) milk

3 tbsp (56 g) hazelnut cocoa spread (I prefer Nutella)

½ cup (120 ml) water

½ cup (84 g) dark chocolate chips

½ cup (84 g) white chocolate chips

4 chocolate sandwich cookies (I prefer Oreo cookies), crushed

½ cup (80 g) vanilla ice cream

MARSHMALLOW FLUFF MUG CAKE

Sick of sharing your desserts with the rest of the family? This fluffy Nesquik cake filled with Nutella and topped with gooey marshmallow is the perfect personalized treat. Make it so you don't have to share.

Yields 1 mug cake

In a microwave-safe mug, add the flour, milk, baking soda, milk powder, sugar, oil and hazelnut cocoa spread.

Using a spoon, mix the ingredients carefully in the mug until they are well combined. Microwave the batter for 1 minute and 30 seconds. Let the mug cake cool for a few seconds and add marshmallow fluff to the top before serving.

PRO TIP: *You can use a kitchen torch to lightly brown the marshmallow fluff!*

INGREDIENTS

½ cup (63 g) all-purpose flour

¼ cup (60 ml) milk

⅛ tsp baking soda

2½ tbsp (18 g) chocolate milk powder (I prefer chocolate Nesquik)

1 tbsp (15 g) white granulated sugar

2 tbsp (30 ml) vegetable oil

1 tsp hazelnut cocoa spread (I prefer Nutella)

1 tsp marshmallow fluff

DULCE DE LECHE CRÊPE

Dulce de leche is a staple in many Latin American countries. In Colombia, it's called *arequipe*, in Ecuador it's *manjar* and in Argentina it is a way of life. This recipe shows an easy way to create this beloved staple with a golden crêpe.

Yields 1 crêpe

Preheat the oven to 425°F (220°C).

In an oven-safe container, add the condensed milk and cover the container with the appropriate lid or aluminum foil. Place the container on a baking tray, and fill the tray with about an inch (3 cm) of water. Bake the condensed milk for 1½ hours.

Once the dulce de leche is done, make sure to remove any burned edges or crust.

To prepare the batter, in a large bowl, add the eggs, flour, sugar, milk, heavy cream and butter. Using an electric hand mixer, mix the ingredients until they're well combined.

In a large skillet on medium heat, add the batter, and let it cook for about 1½ minutes, then carefully flip the crêpe over and cook for the same amount of time on the other side.

Carefully place the crêpe on a plate, and add the dulce de leche to taste. Fold over twice to form the triangular shape and top with whipped cream and some dulce de leche crisps!

INGREDIENTS

1 (14-oz [397-g]) can sweetened condensed milk

2 eggs

1 cup (125 g) all-purpose flour

1¼ tbsp (19 g) granulated sugar

1 cup (240 ml) milk

½ cup (120 ml) heavy cream

1 tbsp (14 g) unsalted butter

GARNISH (OPTIONAL)

Whipped Cream

Dulce de leche crisps

OREO® MUG CAKE

Make the final two Oreos last a little longer by transforming them into a fluffy mug cake. Made with white chocolate, this dessert takes Oreo mug cakes to a next-level taste. You can also add chocolate sauce! Simply melt white or dark chocolate chips and pour on top of the mug cake.

Yields 1 mug cake

In a microwave-safe mug, add the chocolate chips and milk. Microwave the ingredients for 30 seconds and stir to combine; this will make the melted white chocolate base.

Next, add the flour, baking soda, oil and cookies into the mug, then mix well with a spoon. Microwave the batter for 1 minute, then let it cool slightly before serving.

INGREDIENTS

¼ cup (42 g) white chocolate chips

3 tbsp (45 ml) milk

4 tbsp (32 g) all-purpose flour

½ tsp baking soda

1 tbsp (15 ml) vegetable oil

2 chocolate sandwich cookies (I prefer Oreo cookies), crushed

RED VELVET MUG CAKE

It's often hard to find a good cake—they can either be too dry, too sweet or both. With this recipe, you can create a perfectly balanced red velvet dessert. The cocoa powder creates this slight bitter taste, which is complemented by the sweetness of the chocolate chips.

Yields 1 mug cake

In a microwave-safe mug, add the flour, milk, buttermilk, baking soda, cocoa powder, sugar, oil, both chocolate chips and food coloring. Gently mix the ingredients together until they are well incorporated.

Microwave the batter for 1 minute, then let it cool slightly.

Add a small scoop of vanilla ice cream on top (if using) and serve!

INGREDIENTS

4 tbsp (32 g) all-purpose flour

2 tbsp (30 ml) milk

1 tbsp (15 ml) buttermilk

⅛ tsp baking soda

1 tbsp (5 g) unsweetened cocoa powder

2 tbsp (30 g) white granulated sugar

½ tbsp (8 ml) vegetable oil

1 tsp white chocolate chips

1 tsp dark chocolate chips

⅓ tsp red food coloring

Vanilla ice cream, for topping (optional)

APPLE CINNAMON MUG CAKE

This is a homemade dessert with all the flavors of apple pie and none of the struggle. Don't even worry about turning on the oven. This sweet, crumbly mug cake recipe tastes delicious and is ready before you can say, "I want another one."

Yields 1 mug cake

To make the apple pie filling, in a microwave-safe mug, add the apples, flour, sugar, cinnamon and nutmeg. Gently mix the ingredients together. Microwave the apple mixture for 35 seconds.

To make the cake batter, in a small bowl, add the butter, flour, baking powder, sugar, heavy cream, vanilla and cinnamon. Pour the cake batter over the apple mixture. Without mixing the two, microwave the mug cake for 90 seconds. Let it cool slightly before serving.

INGREDIENTS

APPLE PIE FILLING

½ cup (63 g) peeled and sliced apple

½ tsp all-purpose flour

1 tbsp (15 g) white granulated sugar

Pinch of cinnamon

Pinch of nutmeg

CAKE BATTER

2 tbsp (28 g) unsalted butter, melted

5 tbsp (40 g) all-purpose flour

½ tsp baking powder

2 tbsp (30 g) white granulated sugar

¼ cup (60 ml) heavy cream

1 tsp vanilla extract

Pinch of cinnamon

BISCOFF® COOKIE PUDDING CRÊPE

A desert made for champs—hungry champs! This recipe
showcases two desserts: not just a flavorful thick pudding but a crispy,
golden crêpe. Its contrasting textures make for an impactful
and flavorful bite.

Yields 1 crêpe

To make the cookie pudding, in a large bowl, add the water, pudding mix, cookie butter and condensed milk. Using an electric hand mixer, mix the ingredients until they're well combined. Refrigerate the mixture for 1 to 2 hours. In a small bowl, add the heavy cream. Using the hand mixer, whip the heavy cream until it is fluffy, and add it to the mix. Add the cookies, and mix very well. Refrigerate for 6 hours or overnight.

To make the crêpe, in a large bowl, add the eggs, milk, water, cocoa powder and flour. Using an electric hand mixer, mix the ingredients until they're well combined.

In a large skillet on medium heat, pour in the batter, and let it cook for about 1½ minutes, then carefully flip the crêpe over and cook for the same amount of time on the other side.

Carefully put the crêpe on a plate, and dollop cookie pudding on top before serving.

INGREDIENTS

COOKIE PUDDING

1½ cups (360 ml) ice water

1 (4-oz [113-g]) box instant vanilla pudding mix

4 tbsp (60 g) cookie butter (I prefer Biscoff cookie butter)

1 (14-oz [397-g]) can sweetened condensed milk

3 cups (720 ml) heavy cream

11 oz (308 g) speculoos cookies (I prefer Biscoff cookies), crushed

CRÊPE

2 eggs

½ cup (120 ml) whole milk

½ cup (120 ml) water

1 tbsp (5 g) unsweetened cocoa powder

1 cup (125 g) all-purpose flour

ACKNOWLEDGMENTS

Writing my first cookbook is an absolute dream come true! Having the opportunity to share my passion and talent with the world is a privilege that is possible because of the spectacular team and audience that supports me every day.

I'd like to start by thanking my fiancée, Ariana Rueda, who is my biggest fan, meticulous critic, best friend and life partner. My parents, Patricia and Diego, who have filled my life with important lessons and structure that has resulted in the successful completion of this book. My friends who have been there for the entire process since the start, and my cousin, Manuela Caldas, who played a key role in the development of the book.

I'd like to specially thank my incredible editor Marissa Giambelluca and Page Street Publishing, who made this opportunity possible and provided the best feedback and professional insight from the get go!

Special thanks as well to Anthony Nader from 52 Chefs for his incredible photography throughout the book!

Saving the best for last, the biggest thank you to my followers and audience for their unconditional support through this entire journey. You guys are the best! As always, cheers to you!

ABOUT THE AUTHOR

Nicolas Norena, a Miami-based food influencer and entrepreneur, founded The Succulent Bite in 2015.

Nicolas grew up traveling the world and being touched by diverse cultures, foods and experiences. He holds a degree in marketing and business administration from Florida International University. In 2015, Nicolas saw the opportunity to create and put together his company with the vision of touching people's lives through his work. Over the years, he has combined his passions for food, photography and travel to create a now globally recognized brand of mouthwatering food content. He made this possible all while working as a sales representative at a multinational Fortune 100 pharmaceutical company—a position he later moved on from to dedicate his full energy to The Succulent Bite.

Clients of The Succulent Bite include global consumer, snack and alcohol brands such as M&Ms®, McDonald's®, Burger King, Snickers, Papa John's®, Coca-Cola®, Kellogg's, Absolut Vodka®, Bud Light®, Pepsi® and Tostitos® among others, as well as media brands such as Disney+ and Fox. Since launching, Nico has built an expansive network, accumulating several million followers on Instagram, TikTok and Facebook. He shares his most succulent food experiences as well as his travel destinations through his social media accounts. You can follow on Instagram, Facebook and TikTok @succulentbite. You can also listen to his podcast: *The Scoop with Nico Norena*.

Nicolas added to his content repertoire by creating easy at-home recipes that his followers could enjoy and try out with their families. This resulted not only in exponential growth of the brand, but also in dozens of written and photographed testimonials showing appreciation for all the creativity as well as positive impact and energy. Followers of The Succulent Bite are mainly in the United States, but they also reach across all continents.

He was recognized as one of the top 100 influencers in Marketing and Advertising by MARsum—The Global Marketing, Advertising and Retail Conference. He was also credited with the reader's choice of "Best Food Instagram of 2019" by the *Miami New Times*, as well as Johnson and Wales University's ZEST award for best food influencer.

Nicolas has also been featured on programs and in publications such as *Good Morning America, Medium, Yahoo News, ABC News, Insider, Viral Thread, The Food Network, Thrillist, Telemundo, Univision, Ocean Drive* magazine and *Spoon University.*

You can connect with Nicolas on Instagram, Pinterest and TikTok @succulentbite and on YouTube at The Succulent Bite.

INDEX